Downtown

MINNEAPOLIS

Landmarks—Old and New

Minneapolis and St. Paul and Surrounding Areas

Landmarks — Old and New

*Minneapolis and St. Paul
and Surrounding Areas*

A collection of drawings by
FRIEDA RICH
Text by
LAEL BERMAN
Foreword by
CHARLES M. SCHULZ

NODIN PRESS
Minneapolis

ISBN 0-931714-32-X

Nodin Press, a division of Micawber's, Inc.
525 North Third Street
Minneapolis, MN 55401

Printed in U.S.A., at Gopher State Litho, Minneapolis, MN

Acknowledgements

There are many people we'd like to thank for the time, information, and support they so generously provided.

The author is especially grateful to Jean Brookins, Susan Roth, Carolyn Wilson, and Alan Woolworth of the Minnesota Historical Society, whose resources, in particular the State Historical Preservation Office files, were invaluable; Amy Ryan at the Minneapolis Public Library; Iantha LeVander, the Reverend Calvin Didier, Mary Sicilia, Rhoda Lewin, Debra Payson, Gary Criter, Duane Stolpe, Diana Farrell, and Burton Cohen. Gratitude also goes to editors Cynthia Nelson and Elizabeth Knight.

The artist expresses a special thank you to Florence Flugaur, James Richardson, Jr., James Hughes, and Rita Flugaur.

And deep appreciation is extended to the people who made available their drawings by the artist for reproduction in this book. They are:

Governor Al Quie and Gretchen Quie, Minnetonka; *State Capitol Building*

Don and Joan Stolz, Excelsior; *Old Log Theater*

Charles and Jeannie Schulz, Santa Rosa, California; *Highland Park Water Tower*

Ronald and Judy Parizek, Fridley; *Grain Belt Brewery*

Morris and Bess Knelman, Ottawa, Canada; *Walker Art Center and Guthrie Theater*

Robert Wishy, Minneapolis; *Bridge Over Lake of the Isles and Calhoun*

Em Vasek, Sioux Falls, South Dakota; *Minnesota Centennial Showboat*

Gladys Myers, Plymouth; *Milwaukee Road Depot*

Delores Flynn, Plymouth; *Main Street in Stillwater*

Minneapolis Internal Medicine Associates, P.A.; *American Swedish Institute, Our Lady of Lourdes Church, Metropolitan Building*.

Foreword

There is a very honest and human desire to preserve the past. Most of us have a longing to return to the living rooms of our childhood and the streets where we played. We attend reunions, hoping to recapture friendships that meant so much to us years ago, and we return to places that perhaps we saw during the war or college days. It takes a good deal of maturity always to look forward and not to look back. I do believe, however, that there is a value to looking back, even if it is only for comfort. Our society seems not very interested in preserving buildings of great beauty; we tear down marvelous structures and replace them with square savings and loans.

Some people try to preserve our memories with photographs, but the drawings of Frieda Rich preserve and give to us even more. There is a wonderful warmth and spontaneity to these drawings, and for those of us who lived in this area, this collection is of inestimable value. We owe a real debt to Frieda for preserving these memories with her talent. This is the kind of book that one can enjoy alone, and can also use to share with others as we relate to them where we were and what we were doing in those unforgettable days of the past.

Charles M. Schulz

© 1979 United Feature Syndicate, Inc.

Table of Contents

*Building razed.

Preface

The drawings selected for this book are from the artist's collection of landmark illustrations done over a period of time from the late 1960s to the mid 1980s. With the exception of the Metropolitan Building and the old Minneapolis Public Library (razed in 1962 and 1961 respectively), all of the buildings, bridges, towers, and lakes were drawn on site and reflect the artist's impression—given the time of day, her vantage point, and the mood created by the effect of shadows on the texture of a building or on the ripples in a lake. Her medium is the felt tip pen with which she works broadly or minutely, building up tones to capture the character of a structure.

Interesting things happen when an artist sits outside to sketch. Children approach with curiosity and candor ("Are you going to draw *all* those windows?"), strangers feel part of the scene ("I used to work in that building there."), and job offers come out of the blue. While sketching the governor's residence in 1982, the artist attracted the attention of First Lady Gretchen Quie, who commissioned her to draw the State Capitol building for the First Family's Christmas card that year.

For a writer, creating the text for a book of landmarks is like exploring an heirloom-filled attic. Memorabilia abound, relationships unfold, and one discovery leads to another. The fact that Edward Duffield Neill, founder of Macalester College, built the first home on Summit Avenue on land that later became the site of railroad baron James J. Hill's mansion may be merely interesting to the casual reader; to the researcher it's heady stuff. The relationships between people and places are what make landmarks the memorable sites they are, providing the backdrop (as well as the anecdote) for an author's perspective.

We hope the drawings in this book, like pictures in a family album, will evoke memories of time and place . . . and that the descriptions will add to your knowledge of the twin—but individual—cities, Minneapolis and St. Paul.

Alexander Ramsey House

As a favor for helping President Zachary Taylor and the Whigs win the 1848 election, Alexander Ramsey was given the governorship of the territory known as Minnesota. When the young Pennsylvania lawyer arrived in St. Paul by steamship in May of 1849 and saw before him a rough-and-tumble town of scattered log cabins, the appointment may well have seemed more a prank than a prize. But Ramsey made St. Paul his home for the next half-century, serving as first governor of the territory, second governor of the state, mayor of St. Paul, and eventually U.S. senator. Following a stint in Washington as secretary of war under Rutherford B. Hayes, the celebrated statesman returned to his adopted city and the stately gray limestone home he built in 1872 on Walnut and Exchange streets—a fashionable address, to be sure, though not entirely citified, as cows still roamed across the road in Irvine Park.

Ramsey, his wife Anna, and daughter Marion (two sons had died in childhood) led active social lives in the French Renaissance-styled residence with its black walnut and mahogany woodwork, formal reception hall (visitors did indeed leave calling cards), and ornate chandeliered parlor where the family entertained the state's leading luminaries of the day—from preachers to presidents to run-of-the-city politicians.

Ramsey's upstairs study/office was reached by a back stairway, so that farmers or land tenants wishing to discuss business—the practical patrician also owned real estate—could come and go informally, or, if need be, discreetly, without disturbing tea in the library or a party in the parlor.

Marion married railroad land commissioner Charles E. Furness in the home—a major social event of 1875—and following her mother's death in 1884 she became Ramsey's hostess and mistress of the mansion. Her own children enjoyed their birthday parties and other family festivities in high-ceilinged Victorian splendor.

When Ramsey died in 1903 the Furnesses stayed on, and after Marion passed away in 1935 her two daughters Laura and Anna continued to live in the historic three-story home where they grew up and had their coming-out parties.

Few changes were made in the house during the nearly 90 years that the Ramsey and Furness families occupied it. Furniture, books (the governor favored Dickens), and the proverbial nineteenth-century bric-a-brac remain today in the home that was willed to and restored by the Minnesota Historical Society in 1964, following Laura's death in 1959 and Anna's five years later. (The Furness daughters and son left no heirs.)

Tours are given from April through December, with special programs scheduled during the Christmas season. The old carriage house to the west of the main house has been rebuilt and is now a cozy visitors' center and gift shop.

F. RICH

American Swedish Institute

Built as a private residence and likened to a medieval castle, the turreted and towering American Swedish Institute is something of a stunner.

The three-story, 33-room stone mansion at 2600 Park Avenue in Minneapolis was constructed between 1903 and 1908 for Swan Turnblad, the rags-to-riches immigrant who turned a struggling Swedish newspaper into the largest weekly of its kind in the country.

Turnblad and his wife and daughter lived there only a short time, however, preferring instead an apartment across the street, a residence on Stevens Avenue, or the third floor of the downtown Posten building, which he built in 1915 to house his paper, the *Svenska Amerikanska Posten*. In 1929, four years before he died, Turnblad gave the house, the paper, and the building to the American Institute of Swedish Arts, Literature and Science (later the American Swedish Institute) and served as its first president.

Today the institute is both a museum of Swedish-American culture (with a membership of 7,000) and a monument to the American Dream. The 5'4" Turnblad, a onetime typesetter who parlayed pennies and perseverence into a sizeable fortune, spared little expense in erecting his $1.5 million manor, which may have been intended as one-upmanship on the Lowry Hill bluebloods who denied him entry into their enclave.

Designed by architects Christopher Boehme and Victor Cordella, the Romanesque-style building boasts an exterior of cut grey Bedford stone with carvings by Herman Schlink, an architectural sculptor from Winona. Eighteen woodcarvers lent their skills to the interior where, beginning with the two-story Grand Hall entry, panels and sculptures in oak, walnut, and African and Honduran mahogany dominate the walls and staircases. For 40 cents an hour, Swiss-born Ulrich Steiner carved 80-some cherubs throughout the Music Room. He also built and carved the oak and bleached mahogany dining room table, which can seat 24 people.

Vistors to the mansion-museum, a registered historic site, are encouraged to browse through the myriad rooms where permanent and temporary exhibits include work by leading artists of Swedish origin, over 600 samples of Swedish glass, "America trunks"—the potpourri of possessions that accompanied the immigrants to their new land—and memorabilia such as the blueprints for the Civil War battleship *Monitor*, the victorious ironclad vessel designed by Swedish inventor and engineer John Ericsson.

Special holiday exhibitions and celebrations are held at the institute, where luminaries such as President Eisenhower, H.R.H. Prince Bertil of Sweden, and Nelson Rockefeller also were entertained.

F. RICH
6/1978

Bridge Over Lake of the Isles and Lake Calhoun

Picturesque and practical, the bridge over the channel between Lake of the Isles and the lagoon of Calhoun is a concrete example of the stature of Minneapolis as the city of lakes and parks.

Once a marshy swampland where missionaries Samuel and Gideon Pond built their two-room cabin in the 1830s and sought to evangelize the Indians, the celebrated waterways of Calhoun (named for John C. Calhoun, secretary of war under President James Monroe) and the Isles have become home to swimmers, boaters, water skiers, dog sledders, and skaters, not to mention bikers, hikers, and runners, who can be found year-round on and along the scenic paths.

Recreationally and residentially, the lake district in southwest Minneapolis is one of the city's loveliest and most desirable areas. Elegant homes grace the lushly landscaped boulevards where luxury resort hotels in the 1870s and 1880s attracted tourists looking to the lakes for fresh air, cool breezes, and a respite from city noise. The lakes themselves, however, were largely mosquito-infested basins, and it wasn't until dredging began near the turn of the century that the landscape literally began to change.

The transformation to clear, deep bodies of water surrounded by natural park land was incentive for further improvements by the Minneapolis Park Board. The limestone-faced structure pictured here was one of six bridges constructed between 1910 and 1911 for the purpose of connecting the waterways of three of the city's major lakes: Calhoun, Isles, and Cedar. (The water elevation of Lake Harriet was seven feet lower, making a navigable connection unfeasible there.)

A competition was sponsored by the park board with cash prizes of $800, $500, and $200 offered for the best bridge designs. In his book *The Minneapolis Park System*, Theodore Wirth noted that "twenty-five designs were submitted, only a few of which were meritorious in character." Of the few, the design by William Pierce Cowles and Cecil Bayless Chapman was selected for the boulevard bridge and was constructed for $30,000.

Upon completion of the bridge in 1911, the linking of the lakes was celebrated July 2–8 with a panoply of fireworks, concerts, pageants, and parades. On "Children's Day" 30,000 youngsters marched down Nicollet Avenue, and more than 100,000 folks observed the illuminated watercraft that lit up the landscape on the Fourth of July.

Such enthusiasm for a civic event was unprecedented in the city's history—setting the tone, as well as the scene, for future generations of lake-loving Minneapolitans.

F. RICH - '72 ©

Burbank-Livingston-Griggs House

One of the first mansions to grace St. Paul's fabled Summit Avenue was the Burbank-Livingston-Griggs house, built in 1862 by James Crawford Burbank, who settled in St. Paul penniless around 1850 and proceeded to make a fortune in the stagecoach, shipping, and transportation business.

In a boom-time era of industrial growth and no income tax, a man's home was literally his castle, and Burbank's choice of Italianate architecture—a fashionable style of the day characterized by elaborately bracketed eaves and rounded arches—was testimony to his status and affluence. The imposing limestone dwelling with its railed porches and glass-enclosed cupola boasted steam heat, hot and cold water, and rat-proof, brick-lined walls—uncommon technology for the times.

In 1883, seven years after Burbank's death, his widow sold the gracious three-story home to George R. Finch, a dry goods distributor and manufacturer, who lived there with his family for a year before selling it to a railroad vice-president named Thomas F. Oakes. In 1888, broker, banker, and railroad builder Crawford Livingston, founder of the St. Paul Gas Light Company, and his wife Mary (niece to Henry H. Sibley, the state's first governor) acquired the residence and settled in with their five children, giving new life as well as their prominent name to the home that bespoke St. Paul's emergence as a colorful and cosmopolitan crossroad of commerce.

In 1915, one of the Livingston daughters married Theodore Wright Griggs, scion of the pioneer lumberman Chauncy Wright Griggs, and the couple eventually became the home's fifth owners. With an eye for antiques, art, and elegance, Mrs. Griggs transformed the Victorian interior, importing whole rooms of eighteenth-century French and Italian decor, including hand-carved Venetian panels and massive bronze and crystal chandeliers. A departure from this elaborate European ambience was the glass-walled basement amusement room with its piped-in sound system and indirect lighting, reflecting the art deco mode of the 1930s.

When she died in 1967, her daughter Mary Griggs Burke of New York gave the home to the Minnesota Historical Society and for the next few years the residence was open to the public—a stylish setting for cultural and social events. Today the Minnesota State Arts Board occupies the first and second floors and the Junior League of St. Paul is the third floor tenant. The home is listed on the National Register of Historic Places.

Calhoun Beach Club

Conceived as an athletic club, redone as a hotel, and revived as a sports and social establishment, the Calhoun Beach Club on Dean Parkway and West Lake Street has been many things to many people throughout its unusual history.

The nine-story landmark edifice, overlooking the lake whose name it bears, was designed by architects Magney and Tusler and built in 1928—that is, the exterior was erected then—but the stock market crash, Depression, and subsequent membership shortage in the proposed private club caused completion to be delayed about 18 years. (During World War II, when nylon hosiery was hard to come by, a free pair of nylon stockings was a perk for joining.)

Following the war, the club provided a lively social and recreational setting for its members, with summer outings, penny carnivals, style shows, costume balls, and dances on the terrace. But by the late 1940s the fiscal tide had turned. The club went into bankruptcy, and the brick-faced building with the red tile roof was converted into a hotel.

In 1954 the building was bought by Minneapolis industrialist Frank W. Griswold, whose management team, despite the lack of a liquor license, hoped to create a splash. Proms, parties, "sweet sixteen" luncheons, buffet dinners, banquets, receptions, and live entertainment brought a flurry of activity to the ballrooms and beachfront verandas. Affluent Minneapolitans resided in deluxe upper floor apartments. Radio station WTCN and WTCN-TV took over the second and third floors for studio and office space and it wasn't long before television's premiere pitchman, Mel Jass, became a familiar sight, arriving to host the station's matinee and evening movies.

During the 1960s, the hotel became a home for the elderly and was renamed Calhoun Beach Manor. In 1977, however, under the aegis of local developers Gary Benson and Bob Mecay, the building was rejuvenated as a stellar sports and social club, reviving the original intent as well as the name. Handball and squash courts were restored, a swimming pool was uncovered, and tennis courts, steam rooms, saunas, sun rooms, and a jogging track were installed. Refurbished in the art deco mode, the lobbies, lounges, and Solarium restaurant glittered with a eclectic array of accessories that included the hand-painted organ pipes from the razed St. Joseph's church in north Minneapolis and a balustrade that graced the city's old North high school.

In 1987, riding the crest of the fitness wave, the club expanded its facilities to include an aerobics studio, volleyball and basketball courts, and the latest in exercise gear, enabling members to get a state-of-the-art workout.

For residents in the building's 80 apartment units, there's clearly more than a room with a view.

F. RICH

Cathedral of St. Paul

High on a hill overlooking the city, the Cathedral of St. Paul has been a spiritual and geographic landmark since the first service was held inside the still unfinished edifice on March 28, 1915.

Envisioned by Archbishop John Ireland and designed by architect E. L. Masqueray, the monumental stone structure, bounded by Summit, Dale, and Selby avenues, symbolized at its 1906 groundbreaking the strength and rapid growth of a Catholic population in the Upper Midwest.

Prior to its construction the St. Paul archdiocese had been served by a series of buildings dating back to a humble log chapel built by Father Lucien Galtier and 12 Catholic families on a bank of the Mississippi in 1841, strategically located for steamboat access. (A marker at the foot of Kellogg Boulevard and Minnesota Street now commemorates the riverfront chapel that gave St. Paul its name.)

The site for the new cathedral was a practical one. It enabled the structure to dominate the city visually: it was conveniently located within the parish's boundaries, and it was just far enough from downtown to avoid the growing traffic congestion.

Consciously patterned after Michaelangelo's St. Peter's Cathedral in Rome, the landmark edifice, like the State Capitol building across the freeway, is capped by a mammoth self-supporting dome visible for miles. One of the largest churches in North America, the cathedral is 306 feet tall, 307 feet long, 216 feet wide, and can seat 3,000 people. The facade is of St. Cloud granite, topped by a copper roof "greened" by nature's elements.

Although the architecture is considered classical Renaissance, the interior has been described as neo-baroque, with elaborate ornamentation and a sense of "sweep and majesty."

Archbishop Ireland selected Masqueray to design both this cathedral and the Basilica of St. Mary in Minneapolis after seeing the award-winning architect's work as chief designer of the St. Louis Louisiana Purchase Exposition in 1904.

Neither of the men lived to see the completion of their endeavors, since the cathedral's interior was not considered finished until 1953. (Masqueray died in 1917, Ireland in 1918.) Architect Whitney Warren, whose notable works include New York's Grand Central Station and the Biltmore and Ambassador hotels, collaborated with the Maginnis and Walsh firm of Boston for design of the sacristy and much of the interior. Sculptor E. H. Atkins designed the seven bronze grilles behind the alter, renowned for their size, spirit, and three-dimensional silhouettes.

But it wasn't until December 24, 1986, that the sound of church bells rang out from the cathedral's south tower. Breaking eight decades of silence, imposed in part out of economics in the early years, five bronze bells, weighing 17,515 pounds, played to a capacity crowd of worshippers at midnight mass, heralding the eightieth anniversary of the cathedral's groundbreaking.

Como Lake and Pavilion

Bikes, boats, skates, and snowshoes all have their day on or around Como Lake, where generations of Twin Citians have long celebrated the seasons.

The 72-acre lake, located in the eastern portion of St. Paul's largest park, was named by Charles Perry for his birthplace, Como, Italy. Perry farmed the land around the lake in the mid-1800s when the area, site of numerous potato farms, was outside the city limits.

In 1872, looking at the property's potential, the city purchased it from Perry for $100,00, and a board of park commissioners was formed. Horace Cleveland, the well-known Chicago landscape architect, was contracted to design a boulevard and park scheme, but it was Frederick Nussbaumer, the park's superintendent from around 1889 to 1922, who is considered the creative force in the budding of Como Park. His projects included constructing roadways, gateways, and fountains; installing statues, flower beds, and a Japanese garden; soliciting the St. Paul Railway Company to run an electric streetcar line through the park; and building the Como Lake Pavilion.

Located on Lexington Avenue on the northwest shore of the lake, the concrete two-story pavilion was constructed between 1905 and 1907 to replace an earlier wood frame building and bandstand which, according to the park board's 1904 annual report, proved inadequate for the growing number of people attending open-air concerts. The city put in $8,000 for construction, and in exchange for concession rights, the railway company provided another $30,000. A prize of $500 was awarded to a St. Paul architectural firm; however, their blueprints would have put everyone in the red, so Nussbaumer and architect Clarence H. Johnston, Sr., came up with an acceptable design and executed the plans at a cost not exceeding $38,000.

Upon completion, the Spanish mission revival-styled pavilion and its columned promenade, or bandstand (drawn here from the lakeside view), were duly occupied with concerts, theatrical productions, Winter Carnival happenings, and a host of recreational activities centering around the rifle range, warming house, and boating facilities.

In March 1987, the promenade was razed as part of a multimillion-dollar renovation plan for the 450-acre park. The structure is being replicated on its same site, where restoration of the pavilion is also scheduled.

F. RICH

Dacotah Building and Blair House

When W.A. Frost & Company opened for business in the old Dacotah Building in 1974, the Victorian-styled restaurant not only revived a name but also evoked an era.

In the 1890s and for a few decades after, the solid three-story Dacotah, at the corner of Selby and Western in St. Paul, was home to a carriage-trade clientele who lived in fashionable apartments on the second and third floors and patronized William Frost's pharmacy on the ground level. The drugstore also was a haunt of a young writer named F. Scott Fitzgerald, who often stopped in for cigarettes and Cokes while living on nearby Summit Avenue in the summer of 1919.

By the 1940s, however, the neighborhood was shifting. The once splendid Dacotah, with its tile floors and copper cornices, saw a series of transient tenants. No longer desirable dwellings, the apartments fell into disrepair, as did the eventually abandoned ground-floor stores.

Revitalization of the building (the second and third floors have been renovated as commercial condo space) has been a boon to the historic Summit-Hill district, where Victorian once again reigns supreme. The popular Frost eatery has been likened to an emporium "where people can experience the flavor of the neighborhood without knocking on someone's door."

Across the street on Western Avenue, the former Angus Hotel has been renovated as Blair House, a five-story condo complex with a stylish ground-floor arcade that brings the venerable edifice full circle, so to speak. Before it became a hotel, the high-Victorian building with its stone arches and cone-shaped roofs was indeed an apartment house. Local entrepreneur Frank P. Blair commissioned the building's construction in 1887 as Blair Flats. It cost $300,000 and, like the Dacotah, was considered a top-drawer address. Apartments boasted oak woodwork, gracious parlors, large bay windows, and stained glass transoms. To assure uniformity when viewed from outside, the landlord reportedly provided curtains for every window.

In 1893, following its conversion to a residential hotel, the building was renamed the Albion. Transportation tycoon Thomas Lowry purchased it in 1911, and the name was changed to the Angus, after one of his oil wells. He sold it in 1918, and the once regal residence fell on hard times, changing hands over the next half century until it closed in 1971.

Talk of renovation echoed throughout the decade. In 1981, under energetic new ownership, restoration began.

The building is listed on the National Register of Historic Places.

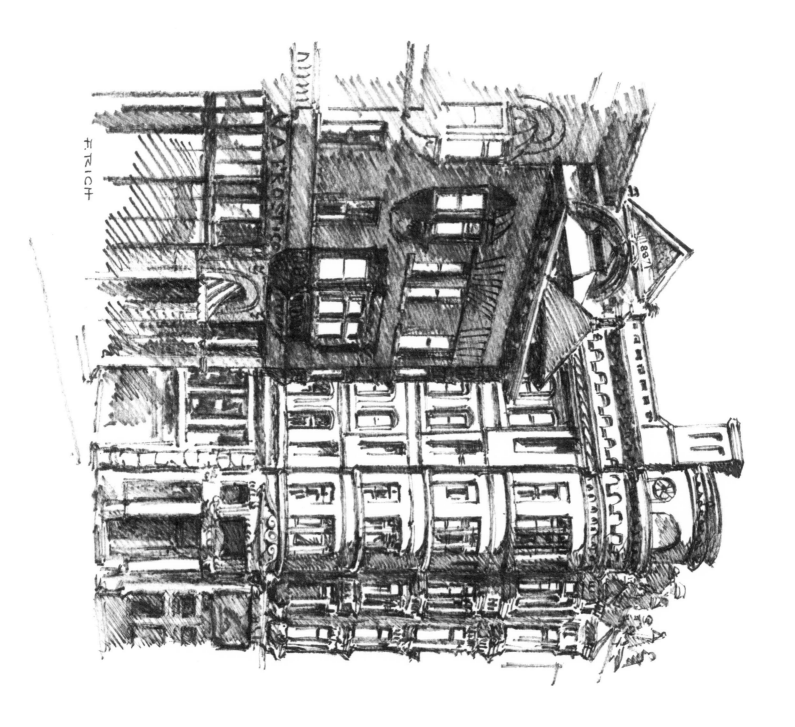

Erd-Geist Gazebo

Romance, restoration, and regional history share common ground in the octagonal Victorian structure that graces the southeast corner of Matoska Park in the city of White Bear Lake, 12 miles northeast of downtown St. Paul.

Site of weddings, concerts, and community celebrations, the Erd-Geist Gazebo—or "gaze-about," as children would have it—is considered the last of the once numerous pavilions that dotted the shores of the lake described by Mark Twain, who visited in 1882, as "a lovely sheet of water . . . utilized as a summer resort by the wealth and fashion of the State." (Twain further noted in *Life on the Mississippi* that there are "a dozen minor summer resorts around about St. Paul and Minneapolis, but the White-bear Lake is *the* resort.")

It was during the town's golden era as a fashionable summer retreat that Bavarian-born Thomas Erd, a well-known St. Paul contractor and stone mason, built the two-story wood gazebo for his daughter Annie and her husband Emil Geist on land adjacent to the Geist's summer lake home. Constructed in the autumn of 1883, less than two years before Erd's death after a long illness, the picturesque pavilion may well have been a father's final fond gesture to his daughter. In his memoir *Life Story and Incidents*, written in 1920, jeweler Emil Geist noted, "Papa Erd . . . had built a beautiful pavilion with which he surprised us, having prevented us from calling on him for some weeks before."

The airy, ornamental gazebo, measuring 15 feet in diameter and 18 feet in height, was enjoyed by members of the Geist family for many years. Ownership of the lake home eventually changed, and in 1974 the gazebo was donated to the city.

Prior to its move to Matoska Park, controversy arose over whether or not the pavilion should be restored and where to put it. Indeed, its renovation and relocation became a cause célèbre for the White Bear Lake Women's Club, who after a false start or two took up the Gazebo Project with gusto and perseverence. A citizen's advisory committee was formed and community-minded individuals also donated their time and money to the effort.

Opinions varied and debates ensued, but civic pride prevailed. The June 30, 1974, dedication program at the park was replete with the Mariner High School band, a Girl Scout flag ceremony, the handling of the deed to the mayor, and remarks from local dignitaries. The gazebo marker was presented and, completing the Norman Rockwell tableau, lemonade was served by members of the White Bear Lake Women's Club.

F. RICH

F. Scott Fitzgerald House

The legend of F. Scott Fitzgerald looms large in the city of his birth. Summit Avenue, the Commodore Hotel bar, and White Bear Lake all lay claim to the celebrated chronicler of the Jazz Age, who with his talented, trendy, and troubled wife Zelda, personified the Roaring Twenties that his writing so deftly defined.

Fitzgerald, whose father was a sometimes salesman, lived at several addresses while growing up in St. Paul, but it is in the row house at 599 Summit that he finished the novel that launched his literary career. On the third floor, during the summer of 1919, the 22-year-old aspiring author rewrote *This Side of Paradise*, the novel he had begun while attending Princeton.

Living on the fringe of the elegant avenue, socially aware Fitzgerald was ever-conscious of money and social position— recurrent themes in his fiction, and it was with a mixture of cynicism and awe that he wrote about the very rich. While he referred to stately Summit as "a museum of American architectural failures," the street was nonetheless the symbol of status and wealth, which seemed to elude his family.

In recent years the row of eight rough-faced brownstone attached dwellings at 587–601 Summit, now called Summit Terrace, have become coveted addresses. Built in 1889, the townhouse-like structures with their myriad gables, turrets, and recessed doorways, are privately owned and/or rented as apartments and condominiums. Indeed, their appeal may have less to do with the eccentric architecture than with the now-fashionable Historic Hill neighborhood and the fame of a former resident, who in a letter to a friend described his home as "a house below the average on a street above the average."

For class-conscious Fitzgerald, who died in Hollywood in 1940, there is a certain irony in the fact that his once far-from-fancy residence is now a National Historic Landmark—listed on the same register as the Summit Avenue mansion of St. Paul's quintessential tycoon, James J. Hill.

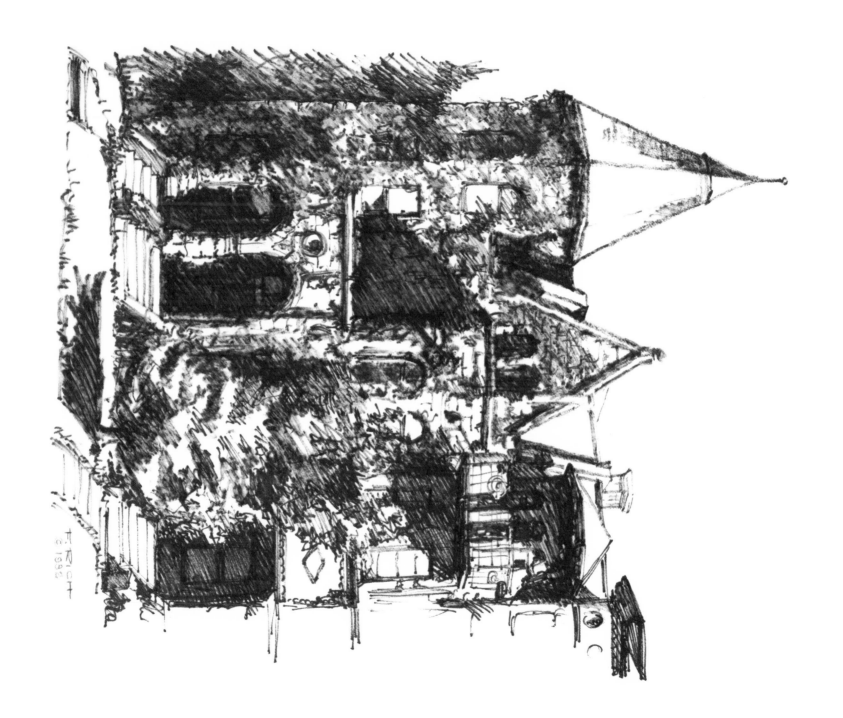

Foshay Tower

Long a symbol of the emergence of Minneapolis as a major commercial market place, the Foshay Tower at Ninth Street and Marquette Avenue was the city's tallest building until the IDS Center eclipsed the 32-story skyscraper in 1972.

Promoted as "the best-known address in the Northwest," the obelisk-shaped office building (which was granted a patent for its unique design) commanded the attention of presidents, premiers, and captains of industry, for its completion in 1929 sparked a three-day celebration, flamboyant even by Roaring Twenties' standards.

The tower, patterned after the Washington Monument with its continuous sloping slides, was commissioned by New York-born Wilbur B. Foshay, a onetime railroad company auditor with a reverence for George Washington, who proceeded to make a fortune in utilities after coming to Minneapolis in 1915. Constructed of the finest materials available at the time, the 447-foot-tall concrete, steel, and limestone-faced edifice, with its legendary top-floor observation deck, was designed by the architectural firm of Magney and Tusler. The art deco arcade boasted terrazzo floors, ornate wrought iron and bronze grillwork, Italian marble walls, elaborate chandeliers, and a gold- and silver-plated ceiling.

The building cost Foshay $3,750,000. His tab for the grand opening was calculated at $116,449.38. The gala—to which he personally invited 25,000 celebrities, heads of state, public officials, and investors—included fireworks, aerial bombs, parades, luncheons, dinners, a 19-gun salute for Secretary of War James W. Good (who represented President Hoover), and the unveiling of the bronze statue *Scherzo* while a bevy of "sea nymphs" danced around the garden court to the music of John Philip Sousa, whose 75-piece band entertained in concert throughout the three days. Foshay also commissioned America's march king to compose the "Foshay Tower-Washington Memorial March."

Within two months, however, the host with the most was broke. Foshay's empire collapsed in the stock market crash, and the rags-to-riches-to-rags entrepreneur extraordinaire was indicted for mail fraud. Sentenced to 15 years in Leavenworth Prison, he served three, pardoned by President Roosevelt in 1937. Twenty years later, Foshay died quietly in Minneapolis, ironically on the 28th anniversary of his buiding's dedication.

The tower, meanwhile, went into receivership and subsequently had a series of owners. Yet its significance and stature have never been diminshed. Listed on the National Register of Historic Places, the monumental bulding—around which a yellow ribbon was tied in 1981 to welcome home American hostages from Iran—remains a thriving commercial crossroad in the heart of downtown.

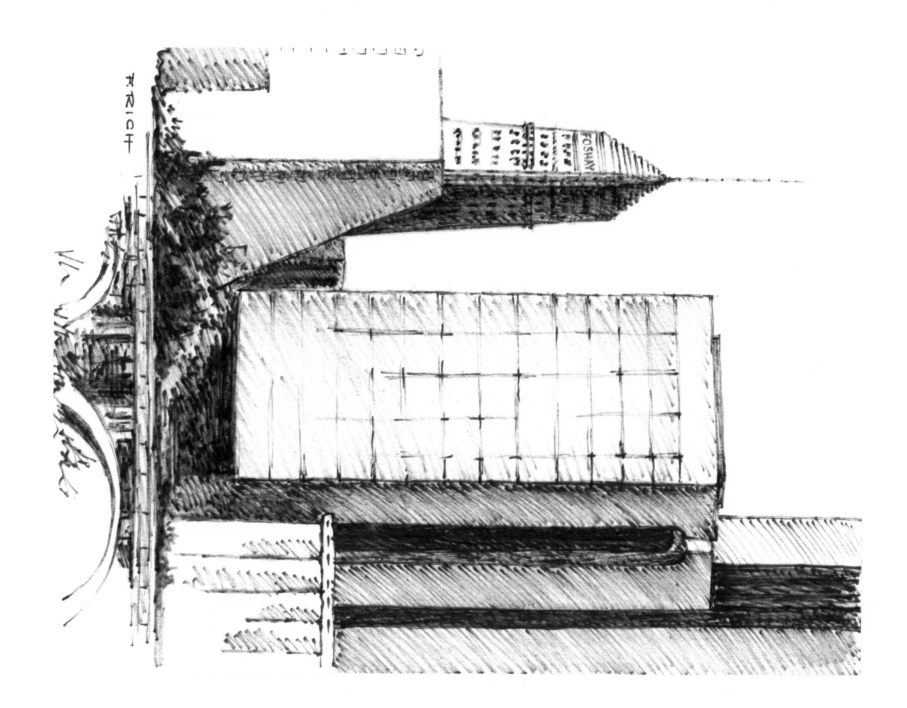

Governor's Residence

The Minnesota State Ceremonial Building, less formally known as the Governor's Residence, was built in 1910 as a private home for St. Paul lawyer and lumber baron, Horace Hills Irvine. The three-story, English Tudor-style dwelling at 1006 Summit Avenue cost $50,000 and was designed by William Channing Whitney, a leading residential architect of the day.

In 1965, as a memorial to their parents (one a republican, the other a democrat), the Irvine daughters offered the 20-room, country manor-like home to the state, which up until then provided no official residence for its top official. Governors and their families had either lived in their own homes or occupied temporary quarters in the city. State receptions took place in hotel suites, public ballrooms, or in the capitol building itself.

With the passage of a bill accepting the property as a residence and for "official public use and state ceremonial functions," Governor Karl Rolvaag and his family became the first official occupants and Minnesota became the 42nd state to establish a dwelling for its governor. (North Carolina was the first—in 1770—while it was still a British colony.)

Furnishings for the stone and red brick house came from a variety of sources. The Irvine family had left some furniture, and other pieces were borrowed from the Minnesota Historical Society, arts organizations, antique dealers, and friends. The Rolvaags promptly gave the rooms a royal touch by entertaining Crown Prince Harald of Norway as their first guest that year.

In January, 1967, Governor and Mrs. Harold LeVander moved in and renovation planned during the Rolvaag administration officially began.

First Lady Iantha LeVander, a dedicated Minnesotan, strongly felt the house and grounds should reflect the state's themes and hues. Adding to the inherited furniture, she artfully incorporated a blue and gold color scheme, and it was also under Mrs. LeVander's guidance that the Minnesota Garden Memorial was created (on the west side of the house) to honor Minnesotans who served in Viet Nam. Artist Paul Granlund's striking sculpture *Man-Nam* was selected from a statewide competition and dedicated in September, 1970.

In 1971 Governor Wendell Anderson and his wife Mary moved into 1006 with their three young children. The third floor attic became a playroom and kitchenette, and in the time-honored tradition of parents everywhere, childproofing the house was a priority. When Governor and Mrs. Al Quie followed Governor Rudy and Lola Perpich in 1979, Gretchen Quie, an artist, converted a storage room to a studio. The Quies also gave J. Q. Public the chance to have an overnight at the residence. Drawings were held 27 times, and the 189 winners had much to write home about. In 1983 the Perpich family moved into the mansion again, and stayed on following the 1986 election. History is still being written.

As one of the Irvine daughters is said to have stated, "No matter which party happens to occupy (the) home, I can rest assured that one of them at least will be content."

F. RICH
© 1982

Grain Belt Brewery

Looming large on the northeast Minneapolis landscape above the east bank of the Mississippi, the Grain Belt Brewery stands as a reminder of turn-of-the-century times when the city shared in the flow of the Midwest's burgeoning beer industry.

The cluster of brick and limestone buildings, whose castle-on-the-Rhine-like facade extends an entire block, is also a symbol of "architectural values as ethnic expressions" during the heyday of brewery construction, when the sought-after architects and engineers were generally of German origin.

With its monolithic arches, attic arcades, and protruding piers, the main building, or brewhouse, built in 1891, is considered the most important major surviving work of Frederick William Wolff. With his partner Louis Lehle, he designed the five-to-seven-story structure combining a potpourri of architectural styles ranging from Victorian to Italianate to Richardsonian Romanesque.

Built on the land of John Orth, Hennepin County's first brewer, the Minneapolis Brewing and Malting Company was founded in 1890, a consolidation of four local breweries. (The Grain Belt label was introduced in 1883, but the firm was known as the Minneapolis Brewing Company until 1967.)

Mergers were a nationwide trend at the time, since heavy competition made it almost impossible for a small brewery to reap the rewards of the growing market. Between 1880 and 1890 the number of U.S. breweries reportedly shrunk from 2,919 to 1,248, but beer production increased 81 percent.

By 1900 the Minneapolis Brewing Company was the major beer producer in the state, turning out 500,000 barrels annually. Prohibition put a damper on production in 1920, and the brewery shut down until the 1933 repeal. With repairs, upgrading, and the post-World War II boom, new sales records were reached in the 1950s.

But the industry was consolidating again, and by 1960 the 400 breweries remaining in 1950 had dwindled to 200.

Expansion was necessary to survive; however the complex on Marshall Street was developed to its geographic capacity, and the acquisition of an Omaha brewery provided only a short-lived spurt. In a vat of red ink, Grain Belt was sold in 1975 to Minneapolis investor-laureate Irwin Jacobs, who six months later closed the plant, auctioned off the equipment, and sold the brand name to G. Heileman Brewing Company.

The bottled-up brewery has since weathered threats of demolition, with talk of renovating the site for office space, a hotel, an art gallery, or a restaurant and retail complex. In Ocbober 1987 the city council purchased the property for further development.

F. RICH

Hexagonal Tower at Fort Snelling

Built in 1820 to establish American authority over the vast new territory President Thomas Jefferson acquired with the $15 million Louisiana Purchase, Fort Snelling—orginally called Fort St. Anthony—was intended to help crush British influence, bolster and secure fur trade for the U.S., and serve as a peace keeper between the Dakota and Ojibway tribes.

Under Colonel Josiah Snelling, the pioneer post took the shape of an irregular diamond to adapt it to the lay of the land on which it stood. The different tower shapes presumably were designed to optimize the line of vision along the angled adjoining walls. The three-story hexagonal tower with its cannon ports and musket slits is one of the oldest buildings in the state and was the least altered of the fort's four original structures when restoration began in the 1960s.

But let's back up a bit.

Lieutenant Colonel Henry Leavenworth, chosen as the yet-to-be-built fort's commandant in 1819, was abruptly relieved by 38-year-old Snelling, who within a month of his arrival laid the fort's cornerstone on the crest of the bluff above the junction of the Mississippi and Minnesota rivers, the strategically located spot recommended years earlier by Lieutenant Zebulon Pike and later confirmed by topographer Major Stephen Long.

Built of limestone quarried from the river bluffs, the garrison was never attacked, and for the next 30 years Fort Snelling was the "hub of the upper Mississippi."

The region's first military post was also a respite for explorers, missionaries, traders, and other travelers who stopped at the oasis in the wilderness for supplies and information. The paintings of artists such as George Catlin and Seth Eastman (later a fort commandant) helped popularize the post as a tourist attraction that drew the likes of Mrs. Alexander Hamilton, widow of the celebrated statesman, who waxed romantic over the fortress, likening it to a castle on the Rhine.

In the late 1840s and 1850s as more outposts developed westward and Minnesota became a territory with its own government, Fort Snelling basically served as a supply depot for other stations. During the two world wars it was an induction and training center.

In 1946 the decaying and deteriorating garrison seemed doomed for demolition. The Minnesota Historical Society deemed otherwise. Through state and federal funding, massive archaelogical and restoration projects were undertaken to return the historic site to its original appearance.

Designated a National Historic Landmark in 1960, the fort became and remains a major tourist attraction with its commandant's quarters, officers' barracks, blacksmith shop, sutlery, and hospital. From May through October, costumed guides reenact life there in the 1820s. The earth-sheltered History Center, built in 1983, is open year-round.

F. RICH

Highland Park Water Tower

Considered the only architecturally significant water tower in St. Paul, the brick and cut-stone Highland Park tower at Snelling Avenue and Ford Parkway is both a bonafide landmark and a lifeline to the city.

The 127-foot-tall octagonal structure, adjacent to a 28-million-gallon capacity concrete reservoir, stands at an elevation of 1,023 feet—the second highest point in the city. A 151-step circular staircase surrounds the 200,000-gallon tank, leading to an observation deck topped by a tile roof and small cupola. Along with a newer blue steel one-million-gallon water tank, the tower is part of the St. Paul Utility's Highland booster station, which serves a portion of the southwestern part of the city. Built in 1928 for $69,483, its construction was an indication of the real estate boom in Highland Park following completion of the Ford Motor Company's Twin Cities Assembly Plant in the late 1920s.

Over the years, the sturdy structure has served as a link to the past for St. Paulites who grew up playing tag, baseball, and golf on the surrounding park grounds. City officials and civic-spirited organizations have also popularized the picturesque pillar. One former water commissioner would invite guests up for lunch and a spectacular view of the metro area. The local business community has raised money for charity by sponsoring water tower runs, races that start and finish at the landmark site. A sketch of the edifice marks the masthead of the *Highland Villager* newspaper.

The tower was designed by Clarence W. Wigington, one of St. Paul's few known black architects. Working under the city architect, Wigington reportedly received little credit for his design, and it wasn't until 1976, nine years after his death, that official recognition was made at a public ceremony at the water tower. During his career in the capital city, Wigington helped design the Harriet Island Pavilion, the Keller golf course clubhouse, Monroe school, and numerous ice palaces.

The Highland Tower is listed on the National Register of Historic Places and has been designated an American Water Landmark by the American Water Works Association. Tours may be taken during the annual Highland Fest celebration in August.

House of Hope Church

From the diary of a seventeenth-century Dutch sea captain came the name of the prominent Presbyterian church that was established by young Reverend E. D. Neill on December 24, 1855.

House of Hope, described in the seaman's journal as a retreat in Connecticut for European travelers in colonial days, seemed the fitting name for a house of worship, Neill believed, where "weary and heavy-laden souls . . . who feel themselves strangers in a strange land" might find refuge.

Neill's meager but inspired band of followers concurred, and made plans to build a "large stone church."

The imposing edifice that today stands on Avon Street and Summit Avenue was constructed six decades and four buildings later—the culmination of a merger in 1914 between the congregations of House of Hope and First Presbyterian Church of St. Paul, which also was founded by missionary-historian-scholar Neill shortly after Minnesota Territory was created in 1849.

Designed by Ralph Adams Cram of Boston, a leading church architect of the day, whose work includes the Cathedral of St. John the Divine in New York as well as the Princeton University Chapel, House of Hope is considered one of the best examples of the Gothic revival style—characterized by a return to "medieval vitality"—for which Cram was renowned.

The building is constructed of Bedford limestone with light buff stone trim. The tower, which unites the sanctuary and the parish house, is perhaps the most dominant exterior feature. A 28-bell carillon, added to the tower in 1923, was enlarged in 1959 to 48 bells and a four-octave range, and is one of the few instruments of its kind in the country.

In 1979 in the church balcony a new organ was installed, notable for its tone, size (four keyboards, 63 stops, and 97 ranks), and the fact that it was designed by the late Charles Fisk, one of the world's great organ builders. The tracker (mechanical) instrument, which took a year to install, is considered his last great work, and at the time of its construction was the largest organ built in this country during the twentieth century. The church sponsors an organ institute every other year, attracting an international roster of teachers and students who come to study with leading organists from around the world.

True to the ideals of founder Neill, ubiquitous in his contributions to St. Paul's spiritual and educational growth, House of Hope maintains a high profile in the city's cultural and civic life. Its Carl A. Weyerhaeuser Preaching Ministry Series has brought in speakers such as Henry Kissinger, Gerald Ford, and news commentator Bill Moyers. The art gallery, originally a cloak room, exhibits the work of Minnesota artists. The Saint Paul Chamber Orchestra has performed concerts in the sanctuary, and singers the likes of Sherrill Milnes have enhanced Sunday services.

F. RICH

James J. Hill Mansion

"Solid, substantial, roomy and comfortable" is the description given the James J. Hill mansion by the *St. Paul Pioneer Press* on January 1, 1891, when the four-story, 32-room home was completed on Summit Avenue, the city's most fashionable street.

Built to specification for the feisty, formidable founder of the Great Northern Railroad, the massive red sandstone dwelling overlooking the bluffs of the Mississippi River was a striking departure from the Italian-villa-style homes of Hill's moneyed Eastern peers. Designed by the Boston architectural firm of Peabody, Stearns and Furber, the house at 240 Summit, often likened to a baronial fortress, characterizes the Richardsonian Romanesque style—named for American architect Henry Hobson Richardson—with horizontal lines, rounded arches, squat pillars, and rough texture. Decor was elegant but understated, with great attention paid to handcraftsmanship ("I want very little stained or leaded glass, but I want it good," Hill reportedly declared) and the most current technology. This was an American-style home for a Midwest-styled magnate: rugged, practical, and fiercely independent.

Including three acres of land, the barn property, conservatories, gardener's residence, and the mansion's furnishings, the "house" cost $931,275.01. (Stonecutters earned $3.50 a day, mortar men were paid $2, and woodcarvers got 40 cents to $1 an hour.) There are 22 fireplaces, 13 bathrooms (the Hills had eight children living at home), a dining room table that seats 40, a reception room that holds 2,000, and a two-story skylit art gallery that held Hill's renowned collection of French paintings.

As to heating costs for the 36,000 square feet of living space, the fuel bill for January, 1894, was $449. Coal cost $4 a ton.

Canadian-born Hill lived here until he died in 1916. His widow, Mary, remained until her own death five years later. In 1925 the Hill daughters bequeathed the mansion to the archdiocese of St. Paul, and for the next 53 years the residence was at various times a school, convent, teacher's college, and conference center. In 1978 the Minnesota Historical Society acquired the property, which was designated a National Historic Landmark in 1961, and began restoring the home to its earlier state.

Tours are given year-round by well-versed guides, who capture the aura of a gilded era and the spirit of a rough-hewn empire builder.

F. RICH
© 1982

Lake Harriet Bandstand

It's a grand old tradition in the city of lakes and parks to park one's self at Lake Harriet on a summer's day or eve and enjoy the sound of music emanating from the bandstand.

Since 1888, when transit magnate Thomas Lowry built the first "pavilion, summer garden and dance hall" and sponsored concerts to boost ridership, free musical entertainment has been a hallmark of the lake that was named for the wife of Henry Leavenworth, Fort Snelling's first commandant.

The newest pavilion to grace the grounds was completed in June, 1986, replacing the previous bandstand that was the fourth structure to serve the city. The first pavilion, designed by architects Long and Kees, was destroyed by fire in 1891; the second building, a pagoda-like edifice with balconies hanging over the water, was the inspiration of architect Harry Jones, and burned in 1903. A year later, Jones created the classically columned third pavilion, which succumbed to a windstorm two decades later. The fourth pavilion, built in 1927 as a temporary facility to be replaced when funding was possible, ironically lasted 58 years. It was razed in 1985.

The fifth bandstand is a single-story, shingle-style building with an "eyebrow" roof and corner turrets, reminiscent of the architecture that characterized the lake's Linden Hills neighborhood at the turn of the century. Designed by Minneapolis architect Milo Thompson, the pavilion is located near the arborvitae on the lake's north shore, the site of the audience area of the previous bandstand.

The 1,500-square-foot concrete stage (10 percent larger than its predecessor) can accommodate 75 performers—50 musicians and 25 dancers or singers—and allows the audience a view of the lake and sky through the pavilion's rear glass window, which also gives boaters a chance to enjoy the ambience.

From June through September, four or five events are held a week, variously featuring amateur and community-based performers, jazz, rock, and country music groups, brass bands, string quartets, and the 44-member Minneapolis Pops Orchestra.

There is "formal" bench seating for 900, although weekend concert-goers have been known to number in the thousands. Indeed, the pavilion's dedication ceremonies drew a crowd of 3,500 well-wishers, who blanketed the beach and boulevard for festivities that included the unfurling of 16,200 feet of aqua ribbon around the 353-acre lake.

F. RICH

Landmark Center

Originally built as a federal courts building, post office, and customs clearing house, Landmark Center in its earlier life was the hub of government activity for the city of St. Paul. A young lawyer named Warren Burger had an office there, as did Congressman Andrew Volstead, best known in the 1920s as the father of prohibition. Presidents Truman and Eisenhower campaigned there, and many a mobster was tried in the august courtrooms, for St. Paul in the twenties and thirties was a haven for hoodlums the likes of Ma Barker, Alvin Karpis (personally escorted to trial by J. Edgar Hoover), and John Dillinger.

Today the renovated five-story neo-Romanesque building is a thriving cultural center, site of concerts, exhibits, lectures, and plays as well as administrative headquarters for the Saint Paul Chamber Orchestra, the Schubert Club, the Ramsey County Historical Society, and other arts and community agencies.

Perhaps most remarkable about this celebrated structure is the spirit and style with which civic-minded St. Paulites rescued it from the wrecking ball when the federal offices moved to a new location in 1967. The statuesque granite building with its twin towers, turrets, and gables was declared federal surplus and scheduled for demolition in 1970. But cries of "Save the Old Federal Courts Building!" echoed around the city. With the help of dedicated historians, architects, and citizens, community leaders spearheaded a restoration campaign that eventually took close to 10 years and $12.5 million before the 80-year-old building reopened to the public in 1978 as Landmark Center, cornerstone of the Rice Park development area in downtown St. Paul.

Owned by Ramsey County and managed by Minnesota Landmarks, a nonprofit, preservation-oriented agency, the castlelike edifice, originally designed by the office of the supervisory architect of the U.S. Treasury, is once again a community crossroads, honored with numerous citations, including a national award from the American Institute of Architects as an outstanding example of adaptive reuse.

Mindful of the building's legends and lore, the Landmark Center Volunteers Association provides tours of the handsomely restored courtrooms and history-filled corridors.

Main Street in Stillwater

The city is the birthplace of Minnesota, and its Main Street can boast businesses that go back generations. There's Kolliner's clothing store, occupying the same building since 1871; down the street, Simonet's Furniture is well into its thirteenth decade; Thompson's Hardware has been a fixture since 1909; and up until it was sold in 1987, the Stillwater *Gazette* went to press each day from the same family that owned it for more than 100 years.

Stillwater does indeed run deep. Visitors to this scenic spot on the west bank of the St. Croix River are quickly caught up in the rough-hewn authenticity befitting a history-proud town that for 50 years was the hub of the Northwest's lumber industry.

Founded in 1843 when John McKusick, Elias McKean, Calvin Leach, and Elam Greeley established a lumber company and saw-mill, Stillwater became the state's first town site and county seat, and built its first courthouse. The territorial convention of 1848 was held on the second floor of John McKusick's Main Street store, where 61 delegates "from the vast wilderness west of the St. Croix" met to set in motion the move to put Minnesota on the map. (The store is long gone, but a plaque marks the site.)

Over the years the picturesque river town, 12 miles northeast of St. Paul, became a popular tourist spot as well as a haven for boaters, picnickers, and other summertime pleasure seekers.

Shops, restaurants, and art galleries opened in stylishly converted buildings, yet merchants have resisted the glitz and gloss that too often tarnish a natural attraction. What could have been cobblestones and kitsch is in fact an amiable blend of riverfront rustic and citified antique. For example, Grand Garage (pictured here), a collection of connected buildings that once held a boarding house, candy company, and auto showroom, opened in 1977 as a restaurant and retail complex adorned with an eclectic array of antiques and period pieces.

Of course the annual Lumberjack Days festival fills the streets with celebrants and souvenirs, but for much of the time Main Street remains Main Street to the 13,000 locals who go about their daily lives grocery shopping at Brine's and Hooley's, book browsing in Brick Alley, and having their prescriptions filled at the corner drugstore.

What distinguishes these and other Stillwater enterprises is the fact that they occupy buildings of historical and architectural significance, preserved and prided by a streetwise citizenry.

F. RICH

Metropolitan Building

Gone but not forgotten, the Metropolitan Building, which stood at Third Street and Second Avenue South in downtown Minneapolis, still serves as a reminder of the ever-urban battle between preservationists and demolitionists.

In this case the wrecking ball was victorious, and the venerable 12-story Romanesque landmark, an "aesthetic masterpiece" and at one time the city's most prestigious business address, was razed in 1962 to make way for the Gateway Center renewal project.

Constructed in 1889 as the Guaranty Loan Building, the granite and sandstone structure, designed by architect Edward Townsend Mix, was hailed as the first skyscraper west of Chicago. Tourists regularly browsed through the interior, rode the elegant wrought-iron caged elevators, and viewed the city's development while strolling on the garden roof to the strains of a string orchestra.

From the stunning central court, a "fantasia in glass and iron," to the fashionable top-floor restaurants where ladies and gentle-men dined and danced, the Metropolitan reeked chic, although its beginnings, like its end, were less than tranquil.

The building's founder, real estate magnate Louis Menage, "disappeared" in 1893 when his Northwest Guaranty Loan Company met with financial disaster and charges of fraud were about to be brought against him. A reward of $5,000 reportedly was offered for information leading to his apprehension, but no arrest was ever made. Menage, who was thought to have fled to South America, eventually returned to the U.S. (though not to Minneapolis), and indictments apparently were dropped.

Meanwhile, the building was bought by Twin Cities transit tycoon Thomas Lowry and sold again in 1905 to the Metropolitan Life Insurance Company.

Ownership changed a few more times before the once grand and awesome edifice was reduced to rubble, and the site became a parking lot. The Galaxy Building now stands there.

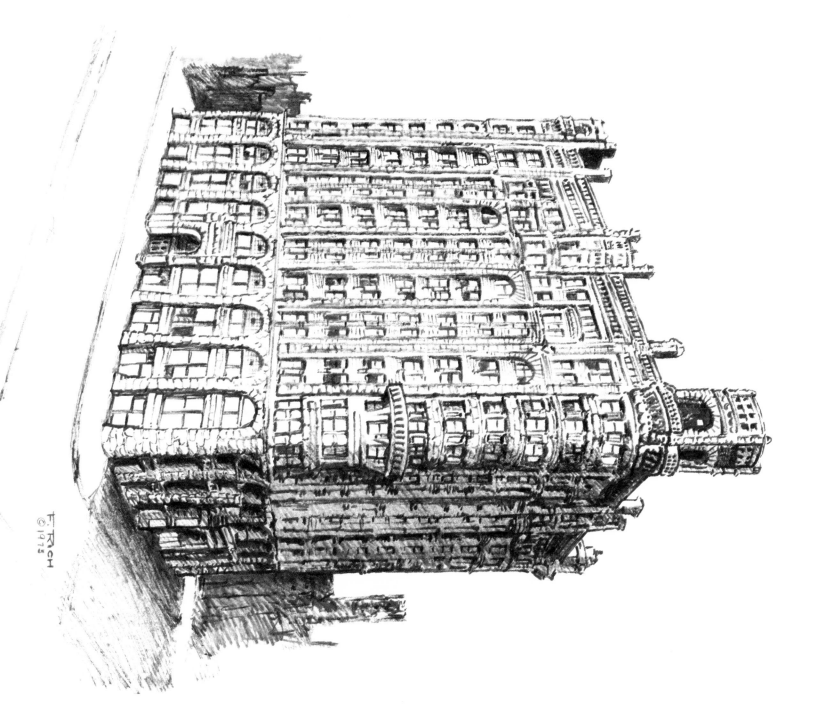

F. RICH
© 1975

Milwaukee Road Depot

Like the old milling and warehouse districts it borders near the banks of the Mississippi River, the 16-acre Milwaukee Road depot site is a symbol of the physical and industrial develpment of Minneapolis during the late 1800s, when trains revolutionized commerce and forever changed the face of the city.

Built to handle 10,000 people an hour, the three-story, clock-towered depot was hailed in 1898 as "one of the finest buildings of the kind in the Northwest." Its patterned marble floors, carved wood ceilings, and detailed plaster walls called attention to a "rotunda that is without doubt one of the most satisfactory public rooms in the city."

Designed by Chicago architect Charles Frost, whose local work included both the Great Northern and St. Paul Union depots, the pink granite and yellow brick station at Third and Washington avenues south was constructed to replace an outdated depot, although the freight house—built in 1879—is considered a part of the earlier structure. Of particular significance is the 625-foot train shed, one of only 12 surviving long-span trussed roof sheds in the country (there were hundreds at the turn of the century), and one of the only remaining ones visible from the street.

The Milwaukee Road was founded as the Chicago, Milwaukee, St. Paul and Pacific Railroad, a merger of several small lines, whose tracks provided the only route between Minneapolis and Chicago in the mid-1860s. Following the Civil War, railroads were encouraged to assist and be part of the city's burgeoning commerce, and turn-of-the-century competition between lines went full steam ahead. The Milwaukee Road reached its peak in the 1920s when 29 trains departed daily from the depot. The station was elaborately remodeled in 1939. The ticket office was modernized, the waiting room's wooden benches gave way to padded chairs, and the Men's Room was redone "with furnishings you would expect to find in your club."

By 1968, with train transportation on the decline, passenger service was limited to five trains daily. In 1971 the depot closed to the public and was converted into office space for the railroad, which declared bankruptcy in 1978.

Talk ensued of renovating the property for shops, condos, a "wellness" facility, and a world trade center. Most notable was developer Harry Wirth's well-publicized attempt to purchase the property in 1981, which ended two years later when he failed to come up with the cash. The site subsequently was sold to other developers.

The depot, freight house, and train shed are listed on the National Register of Historic Places.

E. RICH
©1971

Minneapolis City Hall

In 1889 the Minneapolis *Tribune* stated in its pages, "Minneapolis gives promise of having a hall of justice which will be pushed to completion without . . . carrying down to future generations the taint of boodle and the crumbling evidences of bad architecture and worse construction."

The massive five-story Municipal Building, more commonly called City Hall, has pretty much kept the faith.

Completed in 1906 at a cost of $3.5 million—or 28 cents per square foot—the Romanesque-style edifice has, over the years, had its ceiling lowered, skylights removed, courtyard filled in, ceremonial spaces subdivided, and chamber rooms modernized, but renovation has had less to do with the "integrity" of the structure than with the expanding needs of a growing city's bureaucratic base (a far cry from the building's early days, when to fill the empty rooms, space was leased to a chicken hatchery on the second floor and a horse stable and blacksmith's shop in the basement).

The "granite palace," occupying a square block on Fifth Street South between Third and Fourth avenues, was designed as a city hall and county courthouse by Minneapolis architects Long and Kees, and included in its construction 13,850,000 hard pressed bricks, 60,000 square feet of Italian marble, and 250,000 cubic feet of limestone. The pink granite blocks used for the exterior were carted by horse and wagon from Ortonville, Minnesota.

Built in an era of monumental public buildings, the building's most dominant exterior feature is the four-faced 30,000-ton clock tower, considered the largest working clock tower in the world when it was installed in 1898. Most of the late nineteenth- and early twentieth-century photographs of Minneapolis were taken from its observation deck, 345 feet above the pavement. Above the clock is a 14-bell carillon known for its size, quality, and the fact that for 50 years, beginning July 4, 1912, Joseph Auld, the city's official chime-player, climbed the tower's 447 steps to play for holidays and other occasions. (The carillon was installed with 10 bells, which Auld found inadequate for playing the "Star Spangled Banner" in B-flat, its original key, so he helped promote a fund drive for the additional bells.) Auld's son Edward has kept alive a tradition of note by playing for special events.

Time marches on. In 1976 most of the county offices moved across the street to the new 24-story Hennepin County Government Center. The two granite buildings are connected by an underground tunnel.

In 1983 a master plan for future restoration of City Hall was developed, calling for revitalization of the building's historic beauty while adapting it to practical, present-day use.

City Hall is listed on the National Register of Historic Places.

Minneapolis Institute of Arts

Established in 1883 to "advance the knowledge and love of art," the Minneapolis Society of Fine Arts opened a gallery in six upstairs rooms of a commercial building on Washington Avenue South. Six years and a few locations later, the gallery and its art school moved into the Minneapolis Public Library, then a neo-Romanesque sandstone structure at Tenth Street and Hennepin Avenue. By 1910 the society saw fit to build its own facility.

Civic leader Clinton Morrison, son of the city's first mayor, donated the 10-acre tract of land where Villa Rosa, his parents' gracious home had stood. Thus the Minneapolis Institute of Arts came to be built on the site of the former rose garden of Mrs. Dorilus Morrison.

Designed by the New York architectural firm of McKean, Mead and White, the beaux-arts-style building facing West Twenty-fourth Street was of concrete, brick, steel, and granite— "the most advanced fireproof construction of the day." The lavishly designed interior featured marble stairways, floors, and walls, with parquet wood floors in the then sparsely filled galleries. (For the 1915 grand opening, art from the private collection of James J. Hill was brought by horse and wagon from the railroad baron's St. Paul mansion to help fill the walls.)

Today the Institute claims a collection of more than 80,000 objects. Seven curatorial departments and three floors of galleries, representing the history of art from 25,000 B.C. to the present, feature an internationally acclaimed array of paintings, prints, drawings, decorative arts, sculpture, textiles, and photography. Major works include Rembrandt's *Lucretia;* Goya's *Self Portrait;* the *Doryphoros*, a 2,000-year-old marble sculpture of a Greek spear bearer; Paul Revere's silver Templeman tea service; a rare African Ijo screen—one of seven in the world—and an outstanding collection of ancient Chinese bronzes and jades.

Although a new three-story wing was added in 1927—the work of Minneapolis architect William Channing Whitney— major expansion came in 1974, when the Institute became part of the multimillion dollar Fine Arts Complex, connecting the stately colonnaded edifice with the newly built Children's Theatre and the Minneapolis College of Art and Design.

Designed by Kenzo Tange, the renowned Tokyo-based architect, and Parker Klein Associates in Minneapolis, the superstructure literally opened new doors for the Institute, whose entrance is now on the Third Avenue side, no longer the formidable pillared portico, which, nevertheless, stands as a landmark in its own right.

F. RICH
©1973

Minneapolis Public Library
(former building 1889-1961)

When it was razed in 1961 in favor of a new and more practical building in the newly develped downtown Gateway area, the old Minneapolis Public Library took with it a storehouse of memories spanning more than 70 years.

Built in 1889 on the corner of Tenth Street and Hennepin Avenue, the four-story sandstone edifice represented the evolvement from a private subscription-only collection (housed in the back of a bookstore) to a bonafide "people's" library, free and open to all.

While a public library was the dream held by many an early Minneapolis settler, three men have been credited with its realization: Bayard Taylor, author, adventurer, and crowd-drawing lecturer whose visit in 1859 provided the impetus for the Minneapolis Athenaeum, the literary organization that spawned the Minneapolis Public Library; Thomas Hale Wiliams, the Rhode Island-born lawyer, bookseller, and founding father of the Athenaeum, who in a letter back East described the Minnesota frontier as a place where nearly everyone "smokes, chews, drinks, gambles, or swears"; and Thomas Barlow Walker, lumber baron and art collector, who strived to make culture an equal opportunity experience.

In 1884 the Athenaeum joined forces with the Minnesota Academy of Natural Sciences and the Minneapolis Society of Fine Arts and approached the city council with a proposal to construct a building that would include a public library, a science museum, and an art gallery. Head of the location selection committee was transit magnate Thomas Lowry (who in the 1880s could hardly be faulted for advocating a public building near a trolley line). Securing a site far from the commotion of the central downtown area was also a prime consideration. The upper Hennepin Avenue property owned by Athenaeum member Joseph Dean was deemed appropriate and was purchased at a discount price. Ground was broken in 1886, and three years later on Monday, December 16, the new public library, designed by Minneapolis architects Long and Kees, officially opened.

In *The Library Book*, a marvelous chronicle of the Minneapolis Public Library (and the city itself), author Bruce Benidt notes that the L-shaped structure, which eventually took the shape of a square, had room for 105,000 books on 10,582 feet of stacks made of gas pipe with adjustable shelving. The main reading room on the first floor was finished in mahogany with an 18-foot ceiling, wainscoting eight feet high and 15-foot mantels over the fireplace.

But for generations of immigrants, settlers, students, and scholars it was perhaps the Hennepin Avenue entrance that best bespoke the building's aura and egalitarian intent. Above the Jakob Fjelde-designed seven-foot bronze statue of wisdom goddess Minerva were carved only two words: Public Library.

F. RICH

Minnesota Centennial Showboat

Although cries of "Showboat's comin'!" no longer reverberate along our neck of the Mississippi River, the Minnesota Centennial Showboat is testimony to the times when a unique and picturesque form of theater took center stage in the river towns of America.

Moored near the East River Flats under the Franklin Avenue bridge, the sternwheeler-turned-playhouse is the property of the University of Minnesota, whose theater students present one show a season, mid-June through August, serving as acting company, maintenance crew, lighting technicians, ticket takers, and ushers.

The boat was the 1956 inspiration of Dr. Frank Whiting, then director of University Theater, who envisioned a touring theater as a timely and fitting means by which to celebrate the state's upcoming centennial anniversary. The image of a turn-of-the-century-style showboat entertaining rivertown audiences in 1958 struck a responsive chord in members of the Statehood Centennial Commission who shared Doc Whiting's unabashed enthusiasm and spirit of adventure.

The scene was set, but the logistics were mindboggling. Finding a suitable boat, funding the entire enterprise, and cutting through waves of bureaucratic red tape proved as melodramatic as any potential production.

The plot thickened and the curtain looked doomed to come down when word arrived from Washington that a good old Southern boat was indeed available and plans could go full steam ahead.

The vessel that arrived from New Orleans in April of 1958 was the General John Newton, built in 1899, and recently declared government surplus after years of distinguished service as a freight, mail, and passenger packet whose decks had hosted U.S. presidents Herbert Hoover, Harry Truman, and Dwight Eisenhower.

Whiting and crew spent weeks readying the boat for its new life, which premiered on June 26, when *Under the Gaslight* opened to an exuberant audience and rave reviews. For the next five summers the celebrated sternwheeler played the ports of Stillwater, Hastings, Red Wing, and Wabasha, garnering accolades and news coverage from all over the country.

By 1963, however, towing and maintenance costs had become prohibitive. Touring was no longer practical, so the boat permanently docked in the Twin Cities, where its 210-seat theater continues to attract and delight audiences of all ages. Productions over the years have included *The Count of Monte Cristo*, *Girl of the Golden West*, *Florador*, and *The Bat*.

And the traditional entr'acte olios—song and dance numbers between acts—are still virtual showstoppers.

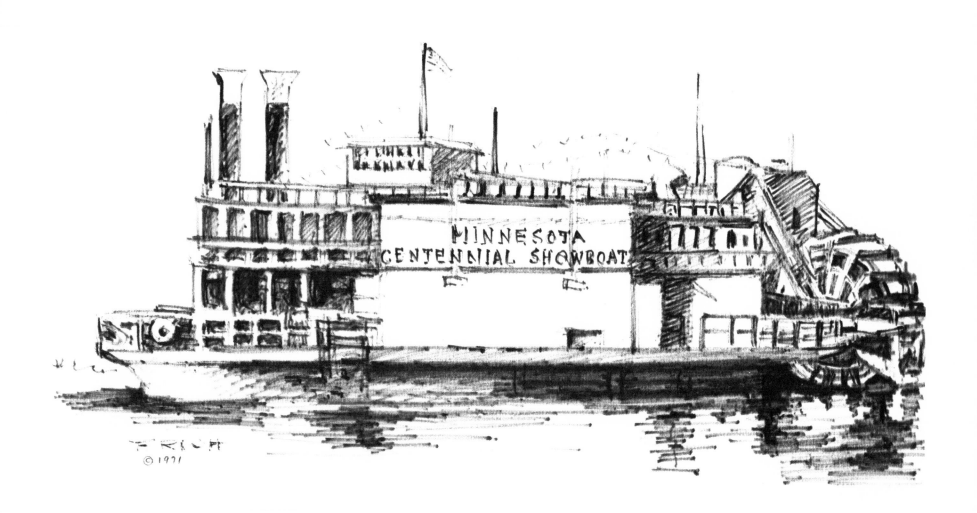

MINNESOTA
CENTENNIAL SHOWBOAT

F RICH
© 1971

Minnesota State Fairgrounds Grandstand Area

Where else but at the Minnesota State Fair can you ride the ferris wheel, eat a corndog, witness high-wire walkers, stock-car races, horse shows, cattle, crop, craft and art exhibitions, and be entertained by world-class performers?

Concluding on Labor Day, the 12-day megafair draws more than a million visitors annually and is the single largest attraction in the Midwest as well as one of the largest expositions in North America.

In 1985 the fair celebrated its 100th anniversary on the same site. The first Minnesota Fair, held in 1859, and those in the early years, had a variety of locations as civic groups in Minneapolis and St. Paul typically fought to have their respective cities be the singular site. In 1885 the Ramsey County board of commissioners donated their 210-acre poor farm to the State Agricultural Society, and the capital city has since been home to the 310-acre fairgrounds located between St. Paul and Falcon Heights.

For any seasoned Minnesota State Fair-goer the Grandstand building is the exposition's symbol of tradition and continuity. The Hippodrome building became the Coliseum, the Mexican village became an international bazaar, but the Grandstand has been the Grandstand since 1907, when the big brick building with the mammoth arched windows replaced the original two-decker wooden structure built in 1885. Bleachers were added during the WPA days of the 1930s and 1940s, bringing the seating capacity to 20,872.

Grandstand entertainment has come a long way since 1899, when the advent of gas lighting made evening shows possible and visitors thrilled to such attractions as sham Civil War battles, fireworks displays, animal acts, and vaudeville revues. In 1962, big name talent began to grace the Grandstand and by the middle 1970s different shows were being presented every night. Performers have included Bob Hope, Bill Cosby, Liza Minnelli, Linda Rondstadt, Julio Iglesias, Steve Martin, and regulars like Kenny Rogers, Helen Reddy, Bobby Vinton, and Willie Nelson, who upon arriving one year was heard to comment, "Boy, I love it here!"

STATE FAIR AUG

F. RICH

Northrop Auditorium

Known as the Grand Dame of Twin Cities performance and lecture halls, Northrop Auditorium on the University of Minnesota campus has long served both the college community and the event-going public.

Designed by Clarence H. Johnston, Jr., and named for Cyrus Northrop, the university's second president (1884 to 1904), who oversaw the development of its graduate and professional schools, the landmark building stands on the north end of the Cass Gilbert-designed mall, where since 1929 it has hosted a veritable *Who's Who* of the performing arts world, including Igor Stravinsky, Sergei Rachmaninoff, Vladimir Horowitz, Paul Robeson, Marion Anderson, and Rise Stevens.

For 40 years, music dominated the 4,850-seat auditorium. Mrs. Verna Scott, wife of Carlyle Scott, longtime chairman of the university's music department, had started an "artists' series" in 1919 that was held in the university's old armory before Northrop was built. (When a funding cutback would have cut short construction of a proper concert stage for Northrop, the redoubtable Mrs. Scott went right to the state legislature and secured the necessary funds.) When she retired in 1944, the University Artists Course was as established as the stately brick colonnaded edifice.

True to her wish, the Northrop stage also became a showcase for opera. From 1945 to 1986 the Metropolitan Opera's weeklong series was one of the biggest cultural events in the Midwest.

The Boston and Philadelphia opera companies have performed here, and the Houston Grand Opera recently presented its award-winning production of *Porgy and Bess*.

In 1974 when the Minnesota Orchestra left after a 43-year affiliation to move into the newly built Orchestra Hall, major decisions had to be made regarding the auditorium's future programming. Given its seating capacity and the size of its proscenium stage, the columned colossus was one of the few facilities in the area that could both comfortably accommodate touring dance companies and keep ticket prices reasonable. The idea of making dance one of its main focal points struck Northrop management as a natural turn.

In 1977 a new "sprung stage" dance floor was installed with a cushioning insulation to give dancers more resiliency. The basket-weave construction was designed by George Balanchine of the New York City Ballet, patterned after the floor of the New York State Theatre in Lincoln Center.

The Northrop Dance Season has proudly presented the Royal Danish Ballet, the American Ballet Theatre, Moiseyev Dance Company, and the Joffrey Ballet, as well as folk, experimental, and "postmodern" dance theater.

F. RICH
© 1992

Old Log Theater

As the oldest continuously running theater in the U.S., the Old Log Theater has been entertaining generations of audiences since 1940, when the fledgling company opened its first season in a converted log stable at Excelsior and Lake Minnetonka. Under the guiding star of Don Stolz, resident director since 1941 and owner since 1946, the fully professional company has grown from a traditional summer stock troupe performing a play a week from June through mid-September, to a year-round operation boasting the best of Broadway comedy and British farce, with shows typically running 12 to 20 weeks.

Over the years, box office hits have included *The Front Page* (featuring members of the working press of the Minneapolis *Star* and *Tribune*), *Mister Roberts*, starring WCCO-TV's Dave Moore, and *The Odd Couple* with the late Ken Senn, who became the first actor in the history of American theater to be associated with the same theater for 25 years. (The same Neil Simon comedy played to sell-out audiences in 1980, when WCCO Radio's Charlie Boone and Roger Erickson took the leads.) Local girl-made-good Loni Anderson of "WKRP" fame had roles at the Old Log as did actor Nick Nolte—Prince Charming in *Rumplestiltskin*—before striking it big in television and movies.

Since its creation, the theater has been funded solely through the box office: no subscription drives, foundation grants, or patron saints. In 1960 the "old" Old Log, now a scene shop and work area, was replaced on the same site by a new structure, suitably rustic but minus the 7-Up cases used as footstools in the early years when water covered the floor of the first five rows.

Indeed, the 655-seat theater, located on 10 wooded acres, has spacious dining areas to accommodate theatergoers with dinner—chuck wagon suppers are a summer specialty—and pre-matinee luncheons. Facilities are also available for business meetings, banquets, and wedding receptions.

F. RICH
© 1993

Old Main at Macalester College

Hubert Humphrey taught here, Walter and Joan Mondale were students here, Alex Haley lectured and wrote portions of *Roots* here, and DeWitt Wallace, founder of *The Reader's Digest*, once took a cow up to the third floor chapel.

It's been noted that every student, staff, and faculty member ever attending Macalester College has either walked through or worked in one of the two Old Main buildings where every office and academic department at one time or another has been housed.

East Old Main, the oldest building on the Grand Avenue campus in St. Paul, was dedicated in 1885 and demolished 101 years later due to deterioration. A 92,000-square-foot library is scheduled to replace the gone-but-not forgotten structure that once housed the entire college.

West Old Main, completed in 1887, originally held 10 class-rooms, a gymnasium, museum, and reading room. Remodeled many times in its academic history, the three-story brick and limestone building, a registered historic site, today holds the offices of the president, the dean of students, counseling and minority programs, and public relations, plus numerous classrooms.

With its arched windows and porticos, gables and dormered roof, Old Main is considered an example of the Richardsonian Romanesque style of architecture, popular during the time that St. Paul architect William Willcox designed the building, and charac-teristic of many of the large homes along neighboring Summit Avenue.

A private, liberal arts institution with an enrollment of 1,700, Macalester College has its origins in the Baldwin School of St. Paul, founded in 1853 by the legendary minister, historian, and educator Edward D. Neill (whose house, built in 1855, was the first on Summit Avenue). The grammar school was named for a Philadelphian, Matthew W. Baldwin, the principal funder of the building that was erected on Fifth and Market Street where Land-mark Center stands today.

In 1874 Charles Macalester, another Philadelphia philanthropist, donated Winslow House, the fashionable pre-Civil War resort ho-tel located near the Falls of St. Anthony, with the agreement that it would soon be developed into a college. The tree-lined Grand Avenue-near Snelling site was purchased in 1883, and the college opened in 1885. Proceeds from the sale of Winslow House funded the construction of East Old Main.

At the building's dedication, the Reverend Neill assured his au-dience that the teachings at the Presbyterian-founded college "would not offend Baptists, Lutherans, Methodists, or Epis-copalians."

F. RICH

Orchestra Hall

"A capacity crowd of 2,573 discovered that the new $10 million Orchestra Hall is a winner," trumpeted *Time* magazine in its November 4, 1974, review of the spanking new Minneapolis concert hall.

Home to the internationally acclaimed Minnesota Orchestra, the rectangular brick, concrete, and oak auditorium, encased in a glass, steel, and aluminum "shell," has been heralded for its high-tech trappings, disarming informality and, perhaps most important, excellent acoustics. Resembling "a mammoth rock fall frozen in the sky," the plaster cubelike shapes that make up the ceiling are superb sound diffusers and have become trademarks of the building, along with the colorful pipes that animate the lobby and exterior facade. The building-within-a-building was designed by Minneapolis architects Hammel, Green and Abrahamson in association with Hardy, Holzman, Pfeiffer Associates of New York and Dr. Cyril M. Harris, a leading consultant on architectural acoustics. The multi-leveled Peavey Plaza surrounding Orchestra Hall is the site of numerous events and celebrations including, since 1980, the annual Viennese Sommerfest.

With a history that parallels the cultural development of Minneapolis, the 97-member Minnesota Orchestra (until 1968 the Minneapolis Symphony Orchestra) traces its beginnings to a 16-man orchestra and a glee club that eventually merged to become, in 1903, the eighth major orchestra established in the United States. Under the baton of Emil Oberhoffer and with the backing of music-minded businessmen led by lumber baron E. L. Carpenter, the orchestra launched it first season at the Exposition Building near the banks of the Mississippi River.

In 1905 the musicians moved to the Minneapolis Auditorium (later named the Lyceum Theater) on Eleventh Street and Nicollet Avenue, where they played for the next quarter century before taking up tenancy in Northrop Auditorium. Orchestra Hall was built on the old Lyceum site, and two terra cotta lyres—vestiges of the theater-turned-salvation center—are ensconced on the lobby wall above the box office.

To date, the orchestra has had eight music directors. Following Oberhoffer, who took the show on the road, touring the country as well as playing Carnegie Hall, Henri Verbrugghen put the orchestra on the air waves. Stricken with a stroke in 1931, the "brilliant Belgian" was succeeded by Hungarian-born Eugene Ormandy, a violinist like his predecessors, who held sway for the next five years. Next came Dimitri Mitropoulos, the mountain-climbing maestro who championed avant garde composers and introduced new music to Minnesota concertgoers. Antal Dorati, 1949 to 1960, enhanced the company's international reputation, and under Stanislaw Skrowaczewski, the orchestra expanded its season to 52 weeks. Neville Marriner, history's most recorded conductor, held the baton from 1979 to 1986, when he was succeeded by Edo de Waart.

F. RICH

Ordway Music Theatre

When the shimmering new Ordway Music Theatre opened its mahogany doors in January of 1985, a high note was reached on the Twin Cities' cultural scale.

The $45 million theatre-concert hall-opera house not only filled a void created when the old St. Paul Civic Auditorium closed in 1980, but added lustre and prestige to Minnesota in general and downtown St. Paul in particular. Named for the St. Paul family whose fortune has long funded the arts, the Ordway is both a hometown happening and an international showcase.

While the glistening exterior of copper, red brick, and glass reflects the architectural history of the downtown Rice Park area, the elegant, finely tuned interior reverberates with sounds ranging from Bach and Puccini to the Modern Jazz Quartet. Audiences here have also applauded soprano Leontyne Price, dancer Rudolf Nureyev, violinist Isaac Stern, the Berlin Ballet, the New York City Opera, and entertainers such as Steve Allen, James Whitmore, and Shirley Jones.

Serving as the principal performing hall for the Minnesota Opera, the Saint Paul Chamber Orchestra, and the Schubert Club, the acoustically engineered Ordway also accommodates smaller, community-based groups and performers in its 315-seat McKnight Theatre, considered a gem of a stage for artists requiring more intimate performance space.

Creating a multi-use building without having it look like a multi-use hall was one of the major challenges met by the project architects, who designed the theatre "as much for the patrons as for the performers." The glittering Grand Foyer and public lobby spaces give theatergoers a chance to see and be seen, while the horseshoe-shaped 1,815-seat Main Hall offers unrestricted views of the performances on stage.

As Benjamin Thompson, the St. Paul-bred, Boston-based principal architect of the Ordway has stated, "Like music, the design of this theatre is at once intimate, then surrounding, classical and yet irregular. It's a rhythmic shape."

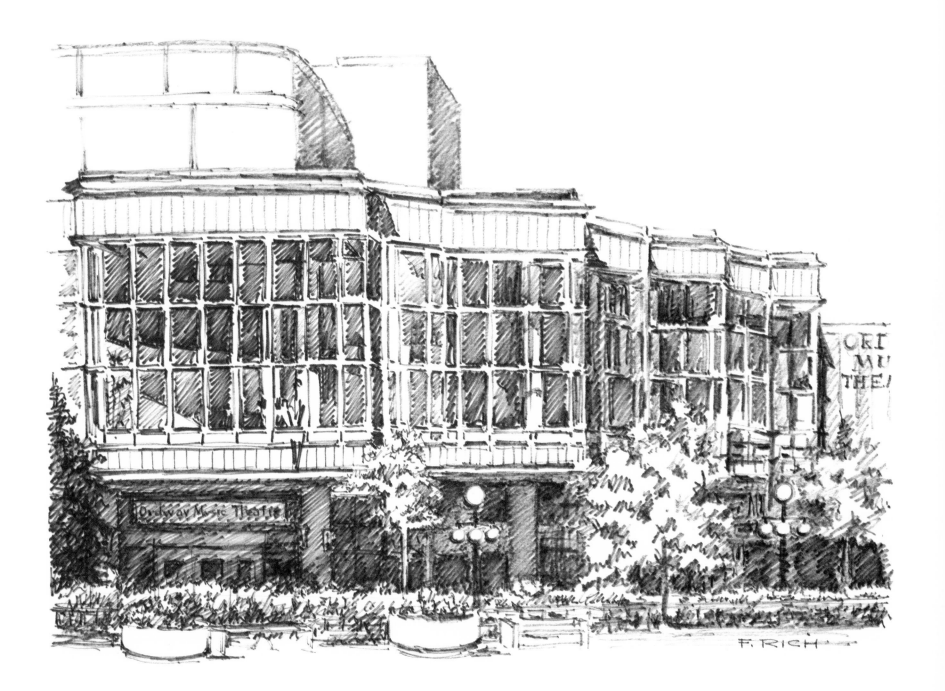

Ordway Music Theatre

F. RICH

Our Lady of Lourdes Church

To many Twin Citians, Our Lady of Lourdes Catholic Church may be best known not for a tower or a turret, but for its tourtieres, the tasty French meat pies whose sales have become symbolic of the parish's perseverance and efforts to keep alive and well the oldest continuously used church in Minneapolis.

Scheduled to be boarded up in 1968, but then resurrected by the development of Riverplace in the early 1980s, the "spiritual home for French-Canadian Catholics" has been valiantly saved and artistically restored by the grace of God, government, and more than a few dedicated souls.

Listed on the National Register of Historic Places, the landmark church at 21 Prince Street Southeast stands in the heart of the St. Anthony Falls Historic District, where the original building was constructed for $15,000 in 1857 as a meeting hall for the First Universalist Society. In 1877 the French-Canadian Catholic community purchased the native limestone structure for a house of worship, and the parish became the first in the United States to be named Our Lady of Lourdes.

To meet the needs of a growing congregation as well as the liturgical requirements of a Catholic church, the original 67-by 44-foot structure had to be enlarged and altered. A bell tower, sacristy, vestibule, and rectory were added, and on Easter Sunday, 1881, a one-ton bell, hoisted the day before, "pealed for all the Masses."

Structural changes also altered the church's architectural style. What had been a rectangular Greek templelike building became a linear French provincial-type edifice with a mansard ceiling and a V-frame beam truss. The circular portion of the nave was modeled after the Chapel Royale at Versailles. A Gothic steeple was added later.

By 1917 the parish was losing its population as the founders passed away and the younger generation of French-Canadians intermarried with their English-speaking neighbors and moved away. French no longer was the primary language spoken in the parish school, and by 1945 the sermons were given only in English.

Today, as redevelopment thrives in the city's birthplace, the little church with the long history is being rediscovered. Visitors take guided tours, which are available to groups by appointment, and parishioners come from "23 suburbs and all the neighborhoods of Minneapolis."

Prospect Park Water Tower

Although it has not been in service since 1953 and was hit by lightning and scheduled for demolition in 1955, the Prospect Park Water Tower, fondly dubbed the "Witch's Hat," still rises dramatically from its hillside setting, preserved through community efforts and re-restored in 1986 with a $130,000 facelift.

Built in 1913, the cast-in-place concrete tower with its peaked Spanish-tile roof, was designed by Minneapolis city engineer F. W. Cappelen, who also designed the Franklin Avenue Bridge across the Mississippi River. Situated on one of the three highest points of elevation in the city, the tower's resemblance to a medieval spire—hence the witch's-hat sobriquet—reflects the popular use of Gothic images for utilitarian structures at that time. The structure was originally conceived as both a tower and a bandstand, but only one concert reportedly was held there. Legend has it that when the musicians marched up the stairs with their instruments, the 60-foot climb to the railing proved less than uplifting. (The conical roof and supports add another 51 feet, giving the tower a grand height of 111 feet.)

Located at Seymour Avenue and Malcolm Street Southeast, not far from the University of Minnesota, the soaring structure is as much a part of the landscape as the picturesque winding streets that have long made the Prospect Park neighborhood an anomaly amid a sprawling urban environment.

The neighborhood landmark also is one of the few original water towers standing today in the metropolitan area. With its newly retiled roof and the current plans to restore its trunk, the treasured tower, according to one public works official, "should last another 100 years."

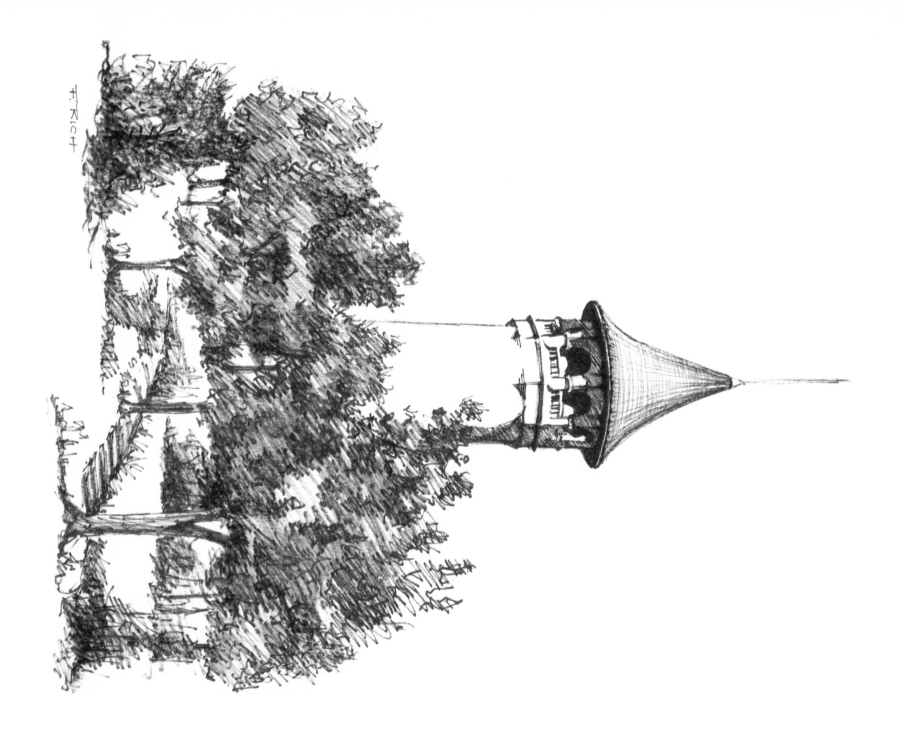

St. Mark's Cathedral

From its site overlooking Loring Park, the Cathedral Church of St. Mark maintains a noble but not uninviting presence. A parish church as well as a cathedral (which it was designated in 1941), the English Gothic edifice has been described as "a big place with a small feel" where the 1,200 congregants have a sense of both community and communion.

Coinciding with the year Minnesota became a state, St. Mark's was founded in 1858 as an Episcopal mission church on Washington and Second Avenue North in Minneapolis. Five years later the small wooden chapel was moved by ox sled to a more promising site, nearer Gethsemane Church, its parent parish on Hennepin and Fourth Street. (Legend has it that the Reverend David Bruel Knickerbacker, conducting a Lenten service in Gethsemane, was interrupted by the frantic gesturing of a man who proceeded to announce, "The church has arrived and we want to know where you want it put.")

But the rapid development of the downtown business area eventually made the new location unsuitable for church purposes. A new residential site was sought, and in 1907 ground was broken at Hennepin Avenue and Oak Grove Street on a choice piece of land donated by the widow of Henry Titus Welles, a pioneer Minneapolis businessman and early St. Mark's supporter.

Edwin Hawley Hewitt, a leading local architect and a St. Mark's parishioner, designed the new house of worship, whose membership included the city's movers and shakers. (The tennis courts and bowling greens that came with the grounds have since been converted to the church's education wing.)

For the building's exterior, Hewitt chose buff-colored Bedford Indiana limestone whose "velvety surface," he was quoted as saying, "enables the designer to secure rich and clean-cut shadows, which, contrasting with the plain and simple surfaces, give an appearance of strength and grace." The sculpted figures on the front facade artfully define the cathedral's commitment to history as well as to things heavenly. Bishops, parish priests, and missionaries who played an active role in St. Mark's and Minnesota's past are depicted along with such state symbols as tepees, gophers, and grain elevators.

The church's pink and buff Kasota stone interior also blends the sacred and the secular. In the Wells Memorial Window one can see basketball players and a wiener roast, commemorating the many activities of the Wells Memorial Settlement House, which evolved from the sewing classes for immigrant women founded by Henrietta Wells, wife of an early rector. The church sponsored the center for more than 40 years, an expression of its mission, "to love and to serve."

F. RICH

Science Museum of Minnesota

In September of 1978 the venerable Science Museum of Minnesota made a quantum leap into the high-tech strata of space age structures. The completion of its $15 million Omnitheater and new museum facility placed the 72-year-old institution in a class by itself, replete with a stellar computer-driven planetarium, the world's largest motion picture system, and a highly technical audio-visual network showing an accurate view of the heavens from any other planet or moon in the solar system.

While films and productions in the 300-seat domed omnitheater are offering close encounters of the clearest kind, the exhibition areas feature classic dioramas, demonstrations, and "hands-on" action exhibits in a blend of science, technology, and natural history.

The three-story science complex, designed by the Minneapolis architectural firm of Hammel, Green and Abrahamson, is the culmination of a dream that began in 1906 when a group of St. Paul businessmen met at the Minnesota Club to discuss the city's intellectual and cultural growth. A gentleman named Charles W. Ames reportedly proposed a series of free lectures on hygiene and sanitation, and industrialist Thomas Irvine pledged financial support. The St. Paul Institute of Science and Letters—eventually renamed the Science Museum of Minnesota (SMM)—was thus created.

In 1965 the museum moved into the newly built Arts and Science Center where its 26-foot-long, 70-million-year-old restored triceratops dinosaur—enshrined on the concourse level—became a time-honored hallmark of the museum's research, resources, and role. Quietly but consistently, the museum gained national stature and recognition for sound scholarly research and innovative participatory programming.

Today more than 750,000 visitors annually partake of the hundreds of programs, courses, classes, exhibits, and special events offered by the museum in both the Arts and Science Center (east building) and the newer "west" building, which connect by skywalk.

A leader in the field of interpretive programming—it has one of the only resident museum theater troupes in the country—SMM also originates touring exhibits, such as the widely acclaimed *Wolves and Humans*, which enjoy a national showcase.

From prehistoric fossils to carboniferous-period plants to a Hmong baby carrier, the museum's collections contain more than 1.5 million specimens of scientific value.

And from a staff of 17 in 1966, personnel has grown to a total of close to 300 scientists, curators, researchers, administrators, artists, and actors.

F. RICH

Southeast Main Street

The neighborhood was the city's first, a rough-and-tumble blend of brick and wooden buildings that housed a general store, saloon, post office, newspaper, law offices, and a fire station. The town was St. Anthony, on the east bank of the Mississippi, where industrious Franklin Steele built the first privately owned sawmill and laid claim to the vicinity with 330 acres of land that he purchased from the government for $450. Subdividing the land in 1849, Steel reportedly noted that the surveyor's map listed the site as St. Anthony Falls, which he regarded as "too big a mouthful for a man to spit out at once," and promptly shortened it to St. Anthony. The road in from his log house became Main Street.

In 1857 the city had a population of 4,689. Its neighbor across the river had 1,300 fewer residents, but the burgeoning west bank settlement known as Minneapolis would eventually absorb St. Anthony to form one city in 1872.

As the united city grew and prospered with industry and an influx of European immigrants, the hub of commercial activity shifted westward "downtown." The buildings along Main Street went the way of outdated enterprises, and by the 1950s the once bustling area was an abandoned relic of a bygone era.

Revitalization of the rivertown site started in the early 1970s. A stone and wood restaurant called Pracna on Main opened where Frank Pracna's saloon had flourished 80 years earlier as a popular watering hole frequented by workers from the nearby flour mills.

Today the atmospheric eatery is one stop among many at eclectic St. Anthony Main, a bevy of specialty shops, restaurants, and theaters ensconced in a series of buildings that include the old Salisbury-Satterlee Mattress Company site, a cluster of three- and five-story structures that were gutted and groomed in 1977 for the first phase of St. Anthony Main's development.

An example of adaptive reuse, the buildings' revival was not an attempt to return them to their original appearance, but to "preserve their character while giving them a modern purpose."

The majority of St. Anthony Main was designed by Benjamin Thompson & Associates, architects of Boston's Faneuil Hall Marketplace and, more recently, our own Ordway Theatre. The Minneapolis firm of Meyer, Scherer & Rockcastle, Ltd. designed the addition that was completed in November, 1985.

F. RICH
©1983

State Capitol Building

Completed in 1904 after nine years under construction, the Minnesota State Capitol building was described at the time as "the latest expression in modern design." Forty-one drawings from around the country had been submitted to a legislative commission who selected the Italian Renaissance-style design of a local architect named Cass Gilbert, who later gained national stature as designer of the U.S. Supreme Court building in Washington, D.C. and the Woolworth Building in New York City.

Gilbert supervised the decor as well as the construction of the $4,500,000 superstructure, and his blending of architecture, sculpture, and painting has been hailed as one of the capitol's most impressive attributes. "In the old days the architect, the painter and sculptor were frequently one and the same man," he once wrote. "There is no reason why this should not be so now."

The structure that stands today is actually the state's third capitol building. The original one, built in 1853, was destroyed by fire, and the second building, completed the following year, proved inadequate for a growing state whose 67-member senate today is the largest state senate in the U.S.

From the gleaming grey-white Georgian marble dome, patterned after St. Peter's in Rome and believed to be the largest unsupported marble dome in the world, to the foundation, terraces, and steps made from St. Cloud granite, the seat of Minnesota government rises 223 feet, extends 434 feet and is 229 feet wide. The high point, literally, of the interior is the fabled rotunda with its Austrian crystal chandelier that hangs 142 feet above the first floor and contains close to 100 light bulbs. Woodwork is of mahogany and Minnesota white oak, while pillars, balustrades, and floors boast more than 20 kinds of imported marble.

But ask any youngster who's toured the capitol to name the building's most memorable sight and chances are you'll hear "The horses!"

The poised-to-prance statues, representing the power of nature, adorn the south facade, accompanied by emblematic figures symbolizing prosperity and civilization. Entitled the *Progress of the State*, the gilded steel and copper quadriga was designed by the eminent American sculptors Daniel Chester French and Edward Potter.

Considered a celebration of civility, the state's chief government building signified to the populace at the turn of the century that Minnesota was no backwater post, but a beckoning and burgeoning state of the arts.

FRIEDA RICH
1982

Stone Arch Bridge and Pillsbury "A" Mill

When it was completed in 1883, the 2,100-foot-long Stone Arch Bridge was hailed as a "magnificent structure," reverentially referred to as The Great Bridge and likened to a Roman viaduct.

Never mind that just two years earlier skeptics had labeled the proposed construction "utterly impractical" or, more to the point, "Jim Hill's Folly."

Nothing succeeds like success. The massive limestone structure, the only stone arch bridge to span the Mississippi River, was a sustaining sweep of architecture conceived by railroad baron James J. Hill, who wanted to improve facilities in Minneapolis for his St. Paul, Minneapolis, and Manitoba line (forerunner of the Great Northern Railroad). Built for roughly $750,000, below the Falls of St. Anthony, the landmark 23-arch bridge, intended by Hill to be "the finest structure of the kind on the continent," weathered close to 80 years of wear before needing major alterations or repairs.

By 1971, however, rail travel was on the decline. Under new regulations, the number of trains crossing the bridge was limited to two a day. The tracks were removed in 1982.

Near the western end of the bridge at the foot of Portland Avenue, a tablet inscribed with Hill's name is testimony to the Empire Builder's pride in the "oldest mainline bridge in the Northwest," a National Historic Engineering Landmark.

Towering above the eastern end of the bridge stands another symbol of the city's pioneering past. Like railroads, lumber, and lakes, flour has left its mark on the face of Minneapolis.

A mighty example of the milling industry's presence is the seven-story Pillsbury "A" Mill, once the largest flour mill of its kind in the world, and one of the formidable structures that for 50 years made Minneapolis the flour-milling capital of the country.

From 1881, the year it was completed, to 1930, the A's output was chronicled with gusto and awe: "16,113 BARRELS OF FLOUR IN ONE DAY" exclaimed one 1905 advertisement, proudly noting that "no other two mills on earth" could equal that sum.

The legendary limestone edifice, designed by noted architect LeRoy Buffington, was built at a time when the 25 mills in Minneapolis were owned by either the Charles A. Pillsbury Company or Washburn Crosby, whose facilities reportedly produced more than one half of the city's two million barrels of flour each year.

Today, with mill activity diminished, the illustrious A is still in use, but mainly for packing and storing.

Pillsbury's
BEST FLOUR

F. RICH
© 1982

Temple Israel

Founded by a charter membership of 22 pioneer German Jews in 1878, Temple Israel was originally called Sharai Tov (Hebrew for Gates of Goodness) and was housed in what was then Center Hall on Washington and Nicollet avenues, thereby becoming the first Jewish house of worship in Minneapolis.

In 1880 the membership built its own edifice on Fifth Street and Second Avenue South, where Rosh Hashanah services on September 5 officially opened the synagogue as well as celebrated the Jewish New Year. Eight years later the wooden *shul* was moved to Tenth Street and Fifth Avenue where, following a fire in 1902, a larger brick building was erected to serve the growing congregation.

The Temple that stands today at 2400 Emerson Avenue South was built in 1928 on land where the synagogue's religious school and community activities building was located, site of what was once "the Smith residence." The architect was Jack Liebenberg, a Temple member whose firm, Liebenberg and Kaplan, also designed Adath Jeshuran synagogue in south Minneapolis and Beth El on Penn Avenue North (now a community social services center).

Liebenberg, who had been the first student to register for the University of Minnesota's School of Architecture, rejected ideas for a Gothic or medieval-style temple, calling instead for a Greek Renaissance look—"the purest architectural style"—which he felt conveyed the rejuvenation of Judaism through the Reform movement.

The five doors leading to the sanctuary were to symbolize the Five Books of Moses, and the 12 interior columns the 12 tribes of Israel. Temple lore has it that when the block of stone with the Ten Commandments designed for the altar was delivered from Mankato, it was cracked and had to be redone. The new one arrived barely in time for dedication services ten days later, and the task of hoisting the 1,000-pound block into place on rollers and a scaffold fell to the architect, the rabbi, and the temple president, in lieu of the workmen who had left for the day.

Over the years, additions to the building have included the S. N. Deinard Memorial Chapel, named for the scholarly and urbane rabbi who from 1901 to 1921 guided the temple and the Minneapolis Jewish community in their growth; an education wing, gymnasium, art galleries, and a library. A $4 million expansion project was initiated in 1986 to include a 250-seat auditorium/theater, additional class and meeting rooms, an enlarged library, and a second main entrance.

"This building must never be completed," the late Rabbi Albert Minda said. "I want this to be an unfinished symphony."

F. RICH

Walker Art Center and Guthrie Theater

Conveniently situated side by side, Walker Art Center and the Guthrie Theater afford visitors a one-stop look at two major Minneapolis attractions that have made the Twin Cities renowned for excellence in the arts.

Although built decades apart—the original Walker went up in 1927 and the Guthrie opened in 1963—the institutions are spiritually connected, for it was on land donated by Archie Walker Sr. that the theater was constructed.

Considered one of the foremost contemporary museums in America, the Walker has its origins in the Hennepin Avenue home of lumberman T. B. Walker, who in 1879 established a private gallery where the "man in overalls [was] just as welcome as the man in broadcloth." The gallery that opened in 1927 on its present Vineland Place site was rebuilt in 1971 and expanded in 1983, the award-winning work of architect Edward Larrabee Barnes. Between the brick Moorish-style exterior and the open, spacious interiors, visitors can view the sculpture of Claes Oldenburg, Alexander Calder, Jacques Lipschitz and Louise Nevelson; paintings by Georgia O'Keeffe, Edward Hopper, Andy Warhol, and Joan Miró; thematic exhibits and premiering shows such as the 1980 exhibition of Picasso's own Picassos.

One special addition is pop artist Roy Lichtenstein's 25-foot sculpture, *Salute to Painting*, installed in 1986 in honor of Martin Friedman's twenty-fifth year as Walker director.

The Guthrie's history is rooted in the Ralph Rapson-designed building it has occupied since the eminent English director Tyrone Guthrie chose Minneapolis for the site of a fully professional resident repertory theater company beyond the mainstream of New York. Modeled after Canada's Stratford Festival Theatre in Ontario, with a thrust stage enabling actors to "play to" an audience semicircling it, the 1,437-seat Guthrie heightened arts awareness in an already theater-minded community, and its presence was considered a coup for Minnesota.

Since opening night May 7, 1963, audiences have watched artful—and often controversial—interpretations of Shakespeare, Shaw, Molière, Miller, Chekhov, and Brecht. Aeschylus got into the act with the 1967 world premiere of *House of Atreus*, adapted by John Lewin and directed by Sir Tyrone (whose last production was *Uncle Vanya* in 1969).

Longtime theatergoers will recall George Grizzard and Jessica Tandy in *Hamlet*, Hume Cronyn and Zoe Caldwell in *The Miser*, and Lee Richardson and James J. Lawless in just about everything. Recent history has included Garland Wright's staging of Cole Porter's *Anything Goes*, and the now legendary *Gospel at Colonus*, that played . . . and played.

F. RICH
© 1973

Wayzata Depot

Nestled near the Burlington Northern railroad tracks and the shore of Lake Minnetonka, the sturdy, single-story Wayzata Depot reflects the image of a turn-of-the-century village train station whose historical significance reaches beyond its quaint and classic architecture.

Built in 1906, the wood and stucco English Tudor-styled station ended nearly four decades of dispute between the Wayzata community and James J. Hill's railroads.

The conflict began in 1867 when the St. Paul and Pacific Railroad (later named the Great Northern) laid the first track—illegally by most accounts—down the main street of sparsely settled Wayzata. As the resort town grew in popularity and population, the boxcars and loading docks blocked traffic as well as the view of the lake. Hotel guests were also kept awake by the switching of train crews during the night and, according to one chronicler of the times, the Great Northern depot's toilet arrangements had "twin privies placed where no one could miss seeing them."

After Wayzata incorporated in 1883, the town sued and won the right to have the track moved. Hill retaliated in a let-'em-walk move, by relocating the station and steamboat landing a mile away, thereby putting a damper on the tourist trade so vital to the town.

In 1905 a reconciliation was reached, and Hill consented to rebuild the depot on its former site. Billed as "the handsomest and best built structure of its kind in the entire Great Northern system," the new station (with indoor plumbing) was completed the following year at a cost of $20,462. The Grand Opening festivities included the empire builder himself passing out small metal hats as souvenirs. While the depot enjoyed a thriving commuter and resort business during the early decades of the century, it wasn't long before buses and automobiles began driving passenger train service into decline.

The Wayzata station closed in 1971, and the depot was deeded to the city. The Lake Minnetonka Conservation District office now occupies the former freight and storage room areas, and the Wayzata chamber of commerce minds it civic business in the stationmaster's quarters. The recently formed Wayzata Historical Society also uses space in the lakeside landmark, which is listed on the National Register of Historic Places.

Tours can be arranged through the Chamber of Commerce, which also hosts seasonal celebrations there.

LOCATIONS

1. Alexander Ramsey House
2. Burbank-Livingston-Griggs House
3. Cathedral of St. Paul
4. Como Lake and Pavilion
5. Dacotah Building and Blair House
6. Erd–Geist Gazebo
7. F. Scott Fitzgerald House
8. Governor's Residence
9. Highland Park Water Tower
10. House of Hope Church
11. James J. Hill Mansion
12. Landmark Center
13. Main Street in Stillwater
14. Minnesota State Fairgrounds Grandstand
15. Old Main at Macalester College
16. Ordway Music Theatre
17. Science Museum of Minnesota
18. State Capital Building